D1537629

OUT OF THE BLUE

OUT OF THE BLUE

PAUL HORSMAN

photography by seapics.com

NEW HOLLAND

First published in 2005 by New Holland Publishers (UK) Ltd
London • Cape Town • Sydney • Auckland

www.newhollandpublishers.com

Garfield House, 86–88 Edgware Road, London W2 2EA,
United Kingdom

80 McKenzie Street, Cape Town 8001, South Africa

14 Aquatic Drive, Frenchs Forest, NSW 2086, Australia

218 Lake Road, Northcote, Auckland, New Zealand

Copyright © 2005 in text: Paul Horsman
Copyright © 2005 in photographs: Seapics.com
Copyright © 2005 in maps: New Holland Publishers (UK) Ltd
Copyright © 2005 New Holland Publishers (UK) Ltd

2 4 6 8 10 9 7 5 3 1

All rights reserved. No part of this publication may be reproduced,
stored in any retrieval system or transmitted, in any form or by any
means, electronic, mechanical, photocopying, recording or
otherwise, without the prior written permission of the publishers
and copyright holders.

ISBN 1 84330 975 0

Publishing Manager: Jo Hemmings
Senior Editor: Charlotte Judet
Cover Design and Design: Tracy Timson
Maps: William Smuts
Production: Joan Woodroffe

Reproduction by Pica Digital Pte Ltd, Singapore
Printed and bound in Singapore by Tien Wah Press (Pte) Ltd

CONTENTS

Chapter Seven

Chapter Eight

Chapter Nine

Conclusion

Introduction

We call our planet 'earth', but over 70 per cent of it is under water, and when viewed from space, 'earth' is blue – a beautiful blue pearl full of life. In fact the blue that we see from space is the oceans: the Atlantic, Pacific, Indian, Arctic and Antarctic.

Life began in the oceans; indeed, the saltiness of our blood is testament to a connection with the sea dating from long ago. More than half the world's human population lives within a few miles of the sea, and for most of us, a holiday often takes us to the sea to swim, paddle, surf, sail or simply gaze out across the waves.

Life, of course, continues in the oceans: from the coldest, ice-bound poles to the warmest tropical seas, and from the surface to the deepest trenches at 11,000m (36,000ft) where no light penetrates, the oceans are teeming with life. There are two vast groupings of marine animals in the world: one occupies the Indian and Pacific oceans, the other occupies the Atlantic and the Mediterranean, separated of course by the land mass of the Americas. There are only a few species common to both areas, chiefly migratory open-water species, however there are representatives of the same genus or type often found in both the Atlantic and Indo-Pacific regions, and this pattern of distribution is believed to indicate that the continental barriers between the two regions are of a relatively recent date.

This book is a celebration of the rich variety of ocean life, from the tiniest plankton to the largest animal ever: the blue whale.

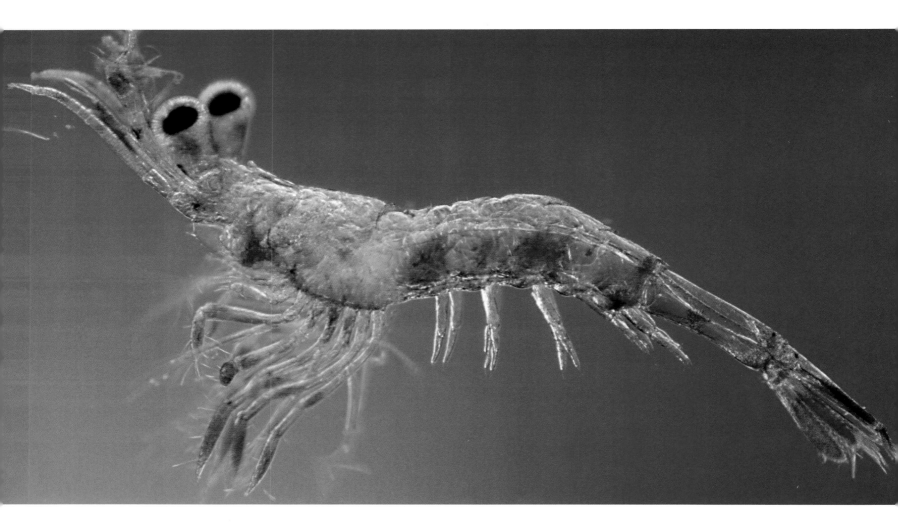

ABOVE Jellyfish are found the world over in all oceans and at all depths. Some can grow to over one metre (3ft) across, others are the size of pennies. They all have tentacles with stinging cells used to catch their prey, which is pushed into a central mouth on the underside. Many species are responsible for dramatic light or bioluminescence displays.

OPPOSITE Moray eels are found in most warm temperate and tropical waters making their homes in small caves and crevices. They are voracious hunters, but will tolerate a small cleaner fish, in this case a wrasse, which picks off parasites and bits of food, even from inside the moray's mouth.

PAGE 8 These euphausiid prawns, commonly called krill, make up a substantial part of the animals in the plankton. They resemble small lobsters and in parts of the Antarctic Ocean can gather in huge swarms measuring several kilometres across. One species called *Euphausia superba* grows to a length of 6cm (2.5in) and forms the major diet of the largest animal alive today, the blue whale, which can eat four tons a day.

PAGE 9 Orcas, also called killer whales, are predatory hunters and found in most temperate waters. They live in family groups or pods and prey on fish, seals and even other whales, usually working together in order to catch their food. They are the second largest of the toothed whales with males reaching a length of 8m (26ft) and weighing up to 7,200kg (8tons).

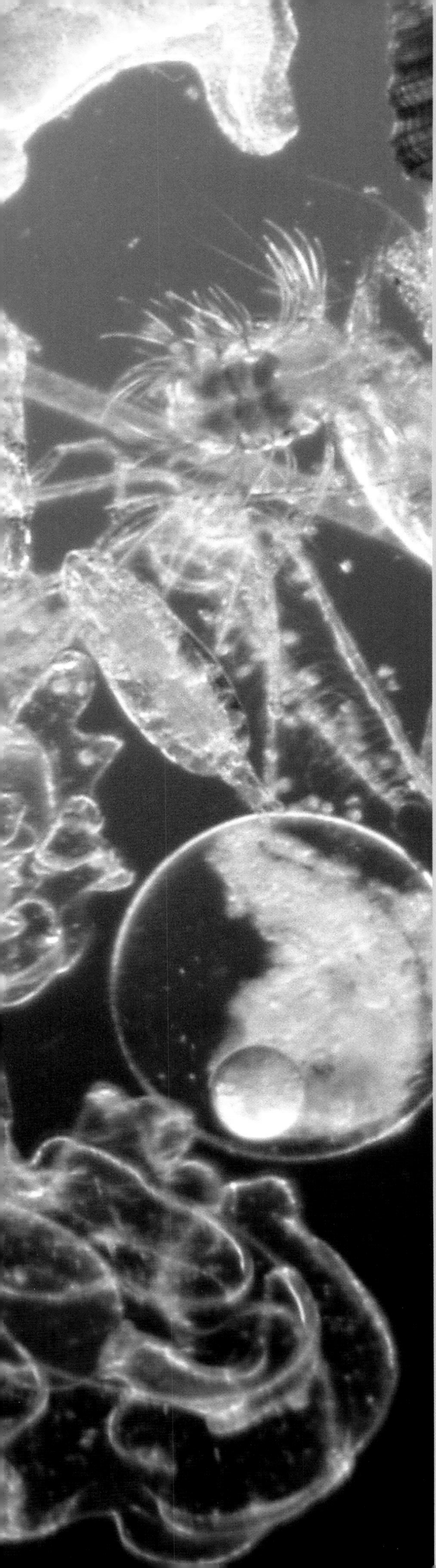

CHAPTER ONE

DRIFTERS IN A SALTY SEA SOUP

The sea, as we all know, is salty. However, this is not just sodium chloride, or common salt, but a mix of salts such as sulphates and carbonates, and of minerals dissolved from rocks over millennia. Generally, seawater salinity is about 35 parts of salt per 1,000 parts of water, but coastal water has a lower salinity due to the input of river waters; melting ice around icebergs has the same affect. Tropical seas are saltier because the sun's heat evaporates the water. The Dead Sea is the saltiest water on earth with around 300 parts of salt per 1,000 parts of water. Salinity affects water density – salty water is heavier than freshwater. Temperature also affects seawater density – warm water is lighter than cold water. It is different combinations of saltiness and temperature, with the wind and the earth's rotation, that cause the great currents to flow around the oceans.

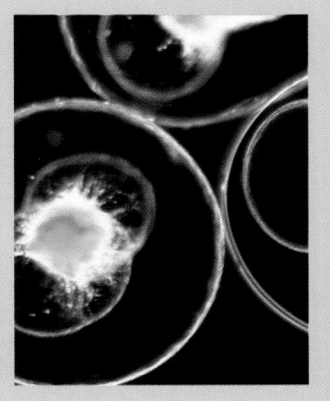

Thousands of tiny animals and plants in plankton make up the base of the marine food web on which the rest of ocean life relies.

Plankton: the Lives of Drifters

Life forms that are not strong swimmers and just drift with the currents are plankton (from the Greek meaning 'that which drifts'). Most of the plankton are tiny creatures, but there are large planktonic animals such as the Portuguese man-of-war or some of the larger jellyfish.

In some areas of the ocean, especially near the coast, a bucketful of seawater will contain several hundred thousand tiny plants and thousands of animals. As you swim in the sea, each mouthful could have hundreds of plants and animals. Emerging onto the beach, some of these would be gasping in your hair or sloshing in your ears. These minute creatures, mostly too small to be seen except through a magnifying lens, are the life-source of the oceans. The salts in seawater make up the nutrients for billions of plants in the sea. These, in turn, are eaten by small animals which are then consumed by larger animals, forming a marine food web.

All natural communities exist as part of a food chain or food web. The sun's light and nutrients enable plants to grow, which are then eaten by animals. Plants are the producers in the chain, animals the consumers. The most obvious plants we see in the oceans are seaweeds that grow in shallow coastal waters although there are some, such as the Sargassum, that grow drifting on the ocean's surface. Abundant though the coastal seaweeds are, there is not enough to form the basis of the entire ocean food web. The real producers or 'grass' of the sea are billions of minute floating plants – the phytoplankton. These are eaten by tiny floating animals – the zooplankton – a relationship that provides the foundation of life in the oceans as zooplankton are then fed on by larger animals which are subsequently eaten by others.

Some animals spend their whole lives drifting at the mercy of the currents, others are only a part of the plankton as eggs or in their juvenile stages, making use of the currents to spread their species to new areas. Eventually these temporary residents in the plankton grow into adults that either swim like fish, or settle on the sea shore or sea bed: crabs, lobsters, limpets, mussels, herring and plaice are just some of the animals that start life as a part of the plankton.

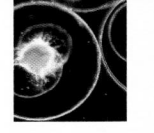

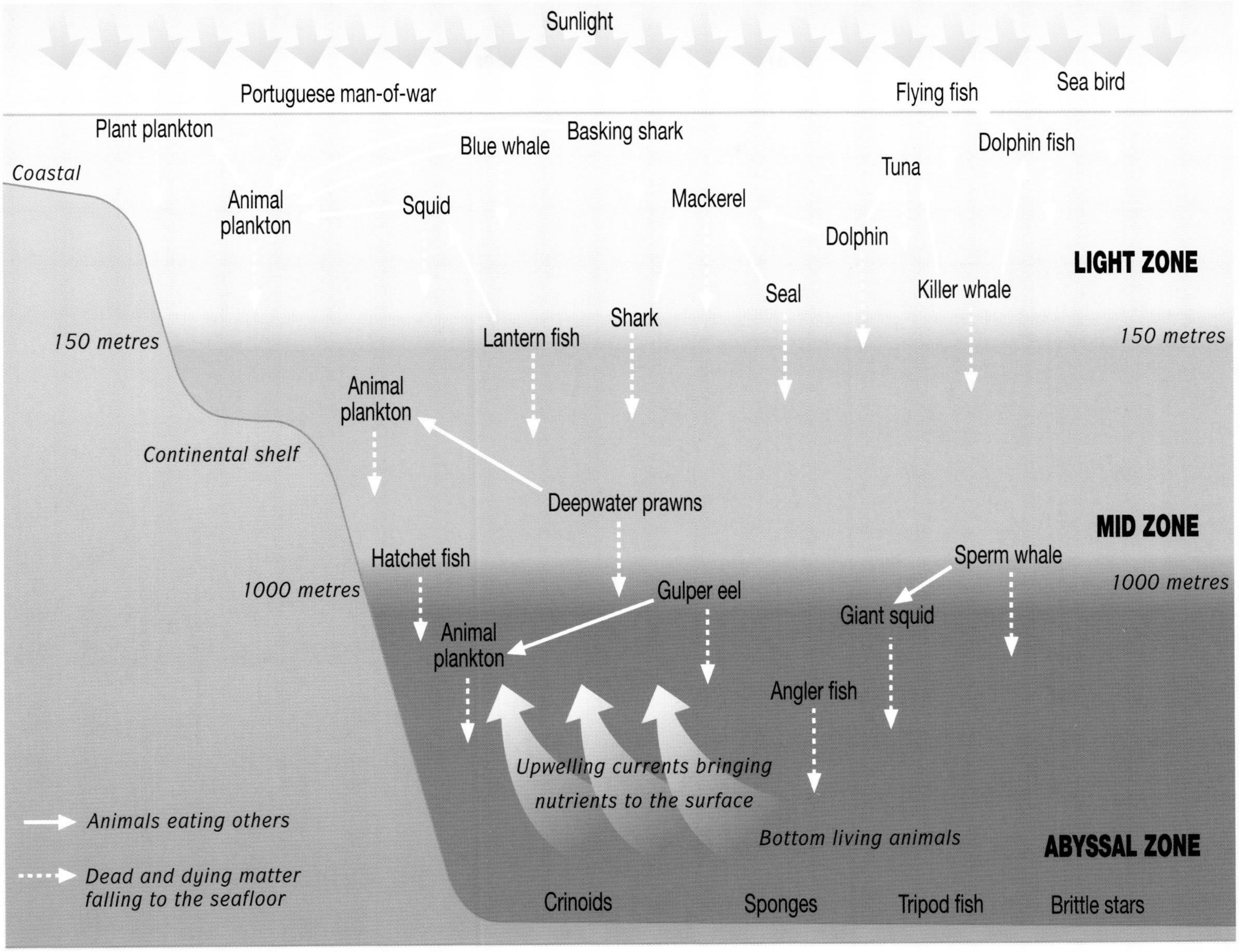

Sunlight

Portuguese man-of-war

Flying fish   Sea bird

Plant plankton

Blue whale   Basking shark   Dolphin fish

Coastal

Animal plankton   Squid   Mackerel   Tuna

Dolphin

LIGHT ZONE

Seal   Killer whale

150 metres   Lantern fish   Shark   *150 metres*

Animal plankton

Continental shelf

Deepwater prawns

MID ZONE

Hatchet fish   Sperm whale

1000 metres   Gulper eel   *1000 metres*

Giant squid

Animal plankton   Angler fish

Upwelling currents bringing nutrients to the surface

→ Animals eating others

Bottom living animals   **ABYSSAL ZONE**

┅┅► Dead and dying matter falling to the seafloor

Crinoids   Sponges   Tripod fish   Brittle stars

Drifting but not Random

Although the plankton spend their time drifting with ocean currents, there is nothing random about their distribution. The oceans may appear fairly consistent, but there are different and clearly identifiable bodies of water. For example, coastal water has nutrients swept up from the sea bed by currents that well up as they approach shallower water, and this is supplemented by the cocktail of minerals – the nitrates, phosphates and other substances – poured in by rivers. The abundance of nutrients enables the phytoplankton to grow and provide food for zooplankton, which also contains the offspring of animals of the sea shore and shallow sea bed, and it is the large amount of plankton and nutrients in coastal water that gives it that grey-green colour, so different to the deep blue of the oceans.

Oceanic water is inhabited by relatively more permanent members of the planktonic community, but a smaller number of plankton overall. As you sail from the coast towards the open ocean, so the large mass of temporary plankton falls, until on the high seas all that can be found are the occasional fish eggs,

ABOVE The food web in the oceans is often large and complex, but fundamentally everything relies on plankton in the transfer of the energy of sunlight to the top predators

OPPOSITE Most planktonic animals are small, but some can join together to form colonies like this string of salps. Salps are planktonic sea squirts, and in species like this *Cyclosalpa* each individual can live separately from the rest, but they can also form long strings, of a metre (3 foot) or more, of many individuals.

young fish and the young of other oceanic animals.

The amount of plankton also changes with the season and time of the day: on land we are accustomed to different seasons during the year, and oceans also experience seasons. In winter many plants and animals die, their decaying bodies adding to the nutrients in the water; then as the days get longer and warmer, the phytoplankton use the increased amount of sunlight and nutrients to grow quickly, thereby providing an increasing food source for the zooplankton that consequently also increase. This is known as the 'spring bloom', the growing season when the numbers of plankton reach a peak. By summer the food is used up and the numbers fall slightly, but in autumn there is another burst of growth as the autumn gales stir up the water, bringing nutrients to the surface. Then as winter sets in the days get shorter, and the populations fall to their winter low, and so the cycle continues.

Plankton soups

At certain times, such as mating seasons, spectacular swarms of plankton can occur. A good example is the Palolo worm, a relative of the ragworms that live in the sand and mud in shallow waters, which normally lives tucked away out of sight in clefts and nooks in coral reefs of the South Pacific. Then, five days after the first full moon in October, a spectacular change occurs and the Palolos emerge in their millions to writhe about in the moonlight in a sexual frenzy before disappearing again. This 'worm night', as it is called in Vanuatu, is a time for feasting both underwater, as fish and other predators take their fill, and above the water as people wade out to scoop up buckets full of the worms. The worms

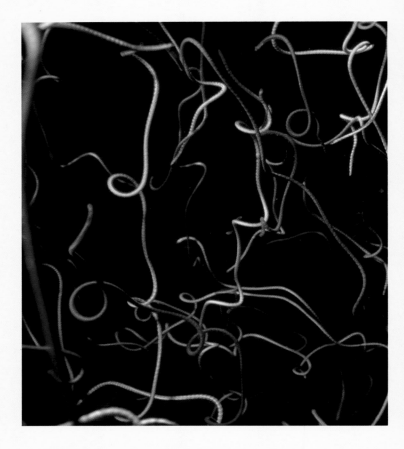

BELOW The swimming ability of these copepods enables them to travel up and down in the water, migrating vertically from deep water to the surface and back.

ABOVE In Vanuatu, 'worm night' occurs five days after the first full moon in October when swarming Palolo worms provide a feast for those both above and below the water.

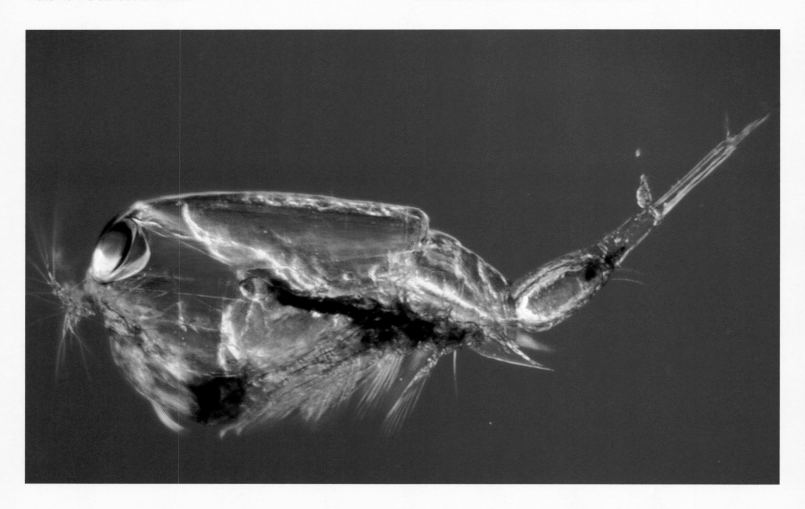

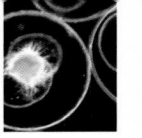

are added to a mix of ground root crop or banana and coconut milk, and then wrapped in laplap leaves and cooked in a pit on hot stones.

Vertical Migration

Although plankton drift this does not mean that they cannot swim and many move up and down in the water on a daily cycle. Dawn finds many animals at the surface but, as the sun rises, they sink and are at their deepest by midday. Then as dusk approaches, they swim back to the surface. Overnight, many are randomly scattered in the water. The distances travelled vary and some larger animals, such as krill, may travel between depths of 600–1,000m (2,000–3,000ft) and the surface while the smaller animals undertake shorter journeys of between 30 and 150m (100–500ft) and the surface.

The reasons for this behaviour are something of a mystery as not all animals migrate. Avoiding too much competition for food could be one motive, but this behaviour also enables the animals to have some control over where the oceans are taking them. At depths, currents often move in different directions to the surface and therefore an animal can execute a roughly square course by, for example, moving from a surface east-west current to a deeper west-east current, thus maintaining a relatively constant position.

Phytoplankton: the 'Grass of the Sea'

Most floating plants cannot be seen with the naked eye, although when millions come together, they can change the colour of the water or cover boats and gear in slime. One species, *Rhizosolenia*, gives the water a yellow colour and bitter taste which herring fishermen call 'baccy juice water'; they know there will be no herring while these plants are around. Although minute, through a microscope they reveal a world of intricate, delicate patterns. Many have cases made from silica or calcium carbonate, which, over millions of years, form chalk deposits. The famous White Cliffs on the south coast of England are made from billions of animal and plant plankton cases.

Plants need sunlight so they must stay near the sea surface hence, to stop them from sinking, many have long spines and oil droplets and some have whip-like tails that beat to move them through the water. Many planktonic animals also contain oil to aid flotation and when large waves break up the bodies of such animals and plants, the waves form froth, called spume, on the water or beach.

BELOW Long spines and whip-like tails keep the phytoplankton in sunlit surface waters. Although most phytoplankton are less than the width of a human hair, some can form chains a few centimetres long.

Red Tides

Large concentrations of plankton sometimes change the appearance of the water, creating red tides. This can happen when organisms are caught where two currents meet and the water sinks forming a down-welling. A combination of the organisms swimming upwards and the water moving downwards concentrates the population which is often seen in lines or windrows on the surface. Under the right conditions with abundant nutrients, a red tide may persist for a week or two. The Red Sea is so named due to the frequent appearance of red tides, but they occur world-wide.

Red tides can be lethal and cause mass kills of marine animals. This can happen after all the nutrients have been used up or if conditions suddenly change and the whole plankton population dies at once. The millions of decomposing bodies use up oxygen in the water, suffocating any other animals. In 1977 an area of over 14,000 square km (5,400 square miles) off New Jersey, USA lost most of its oxygen following a red tide, which killed many marine animals, especially those living on the seabed, such as clams and mussels, that could not escape.

Several species such as *Gymnodinium* and *Gonyaulax* can also kill directly because of poisons in their bodies; some kill fish, others affect warm-blooded animals. Part of Florida's west coast is known for extensive fish kills caused by red tides of the species *Gymnodinium breve*, which makes the water look oily. The organism, taken in with the water

ABOVE In a red tide the water often has the appearance of rust or paint, but the colours vary according to the species responsible, with shades of red, pink, violet, orange, yellow, blue, green or brown being most common.

through the fish's mouth, breaks up in the gills and the poison is released into the blood stream causing the fish's red blood cells to burst. These blood cells, as in human blood, carry oxygen around the body; without these, the body cannot get enough oxygen and the animal suffocates. Florida's tourist trade has suffered due to piles of dead fish being washed up on the shores as well as people exposed to sea-spray suffering from respiratory irritation.

Gonyaulax has a poison that affects warm-blooded animals and causes 'paralytic shellfish poisoning' that affects the nerves and can lead to paralysis and death. Some fish are also affected, but not shellfish such as clams and mussels, and the poison can accumulate in their bodies. In extreme cases, if even just a few infected shellfish are eaten by humans they may prove to be fatal. Unfortunately, poisoned shellfish appear normal so there is no indication of the potential danger. Paralytic shellfish poisoning occurs world-wide, but especially along the coasts of west and northeast North America, north-western Europe and the British Isles, around Japan, in the Bay of Fundy and the St Lawrence river estuary in Canada. Annual blooms of *Gonyaulax* result in areas being closed to shellfish harvesting.

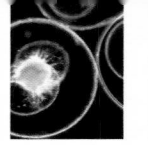

Zooplankton

Although many of the animals in the plankton are the eggs and offspring of larger animals, there are many that spend their whole lives drifting. They include the simplest animals, made up of a single cell, and the more complex. In fact, most animal groups are represented in the plankton.

Most people have heard of or seen jellyfish; they are found the world over, some as big as footballs, others the size of pennies. Their close relatives include anemones that decorate pier piles, harbour walls and rocky shores and corals.

Some animals, like comb jellies or sea gooseberries, are unique to the marine plankton. When washed up on beaches they look like insignificant blobs of transparent jelly; under water, however, they appear magical with their eight rows of hairs or cilia, looking like combs (hence their common name) beating synchronously, so they shimmer when the light catches. They range from pea sized to golf ball-sized, though the flat Venus' girdle, *Cestum,* can grow to over 1m (40in).

The crustacea – crab and shrimp-like animals – are the main food of many larger animals and the largest animals – the great whales – consume some, like the euphausiid krill. There are many different body shapes, including some with spines and long flattened limbs for swimming. Krill look like small lobsters and have light-producing organs called photophores on their lower sides and one species, *Euphausia superba,* can grow to 6cm (2½ inches) and lives in large swarms covering several square km. Such swarms look like constantly moving clouds in the water, with concentrations of over 60,000 animals per cubic metre. A blue whale may consume a ton of krill at one feeding and make up to four such feedings a day.

ABOVE RIGHT Zooplankton contains many animals although some are only represented by the eggs or larval stages. There are jellyfish (coelenterates), comb-jellies (ctenophores), worms (annelids), shell-fish (molluscs), shrimps and crabs (crustacea), sea spiders (pycnogonids), mites (acari), starfish and sea urchins (echinoderms), sea mats (bryozoa), arrow worms (chaetognaths), animals that have a simple backbone (cephalo-chordates) and those with a more advanced backbone (vertebrates).

RIGHT Comb-jellies or sea gooseberries live their entire lives as part of the plankton. They swim using the synchronous beating of hairs around their bodies and catch food on long tentacles.

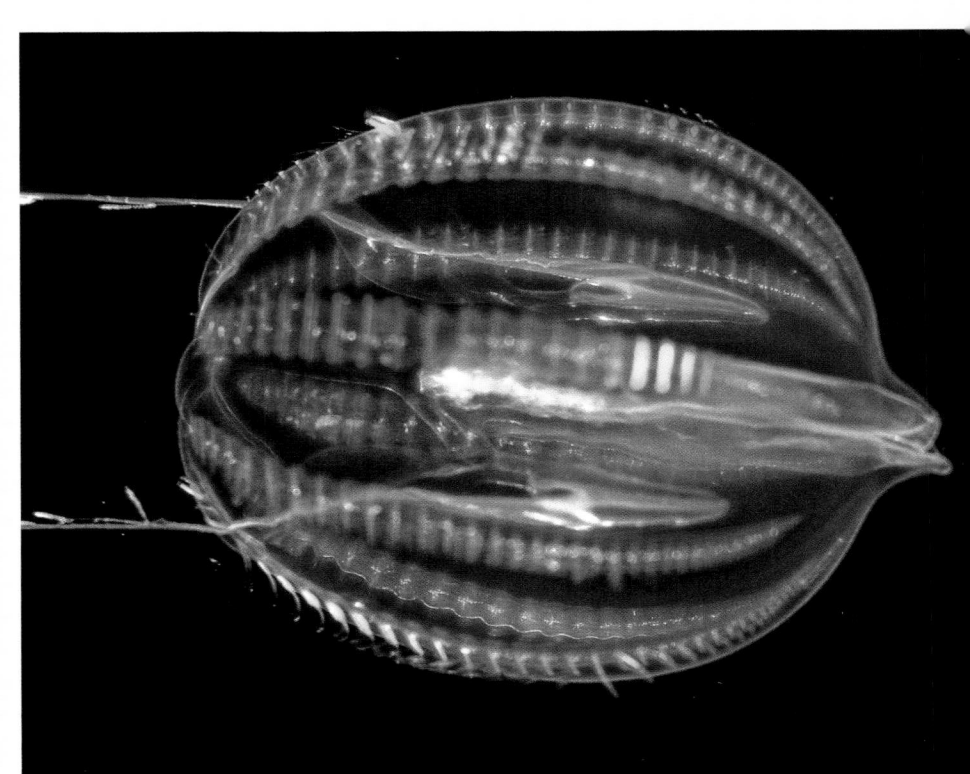

The Right Way Up

Orientation in the water is important. This might seem obvious, but animals do need to know which is up and which down. We know this due to the balance organs in our inner ears, and many marine creatures also have similar balance organs. Those of the jellyfish consist of little chambers, each with a grain of limestone inside that sits on sensitive nerve hairs. It is like a ball in a bowl: when the animal is the right way up the grain is on the bottom, but when it is upside down it rolls to the top. In the opossum shrimps, the grain in their balance organ is made from calcium fluoride.

Copepods

One group of crustacea – the copepods – are almost entirely planktonic, and are probably the most common invertebrate animal on the earth. They are hugely important to the marine food web and form the basic diet of hundreds of other marine creatures. Some are carnivorous and even cannibalistic, so taking advantage of a great abundance of their own kind. But most copepods are herbivores filtering out microscopic plants from the water. In this way these animals fulfil the niche occupied on land by the large grazing animals, such as zebra and wildebeest. Many copepods are responsible for dramatic displays of bioluminescence in the water sometimes seen as sparks of sapphire blue light emanating from the hands and feet of swimmers in the sea at night, especially in the spring. Often trails of fish or dolphins as long as 30 or 50m (100-160ft), can be seen as startling sprays of light in the water.

There are many ways that copepods play their role in the marine food web: fish, such as herring, when shoaling in their thousands, snap up millions of copepods – but fish are not the only predators, and anemones, jellyfish and corals catch these animals using stinging cells on their tentacles. As a copepod brushes against the tentacles, the stinging cells are fired and inject poison or simply wrap the helpless animal up before passing it to the mouth, which is usually in the centre of the ring of tentacles.

Although copepods are consumed in their millions, their numbers usually remain sufficient as they breed rapidly and enough young survive to adulthood to maintain the population which, of course in turn, helps to maintain populations of other larger marine creatures.

Shellfish and Surface Drifters

Other creatures that at first one might think could not possibly drift, are those with shells – the shellfish or molluscs. Apart from the offspring of such animals as mussels, snails, cockles and scallops, there are adult shellfish that, complete with shell, live in the open oceans. Many of these swimming snails are predatory, feeding on small fish and other planktonic

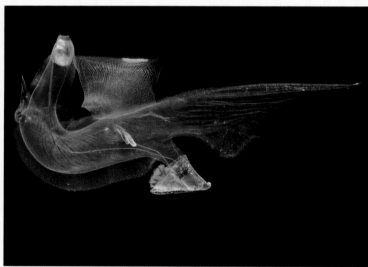

ABOVE TOP Crustaceans make up a substantial part of the plankton soup. Krill look like small lobsters, while the mysids, or opossum shrimps – so called because they carry their young in a pouch – have balance organs in their tails so they can orientate in the water.

ABOVE Planktonic snails have a shell that is so light it looks like glass. The foot of the snail has evolved into large 'wings' for swimming. In this carnivorous *Carinaria* snail, the shell is a very small transparent triangle beneath the body.

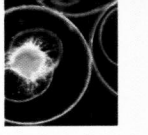

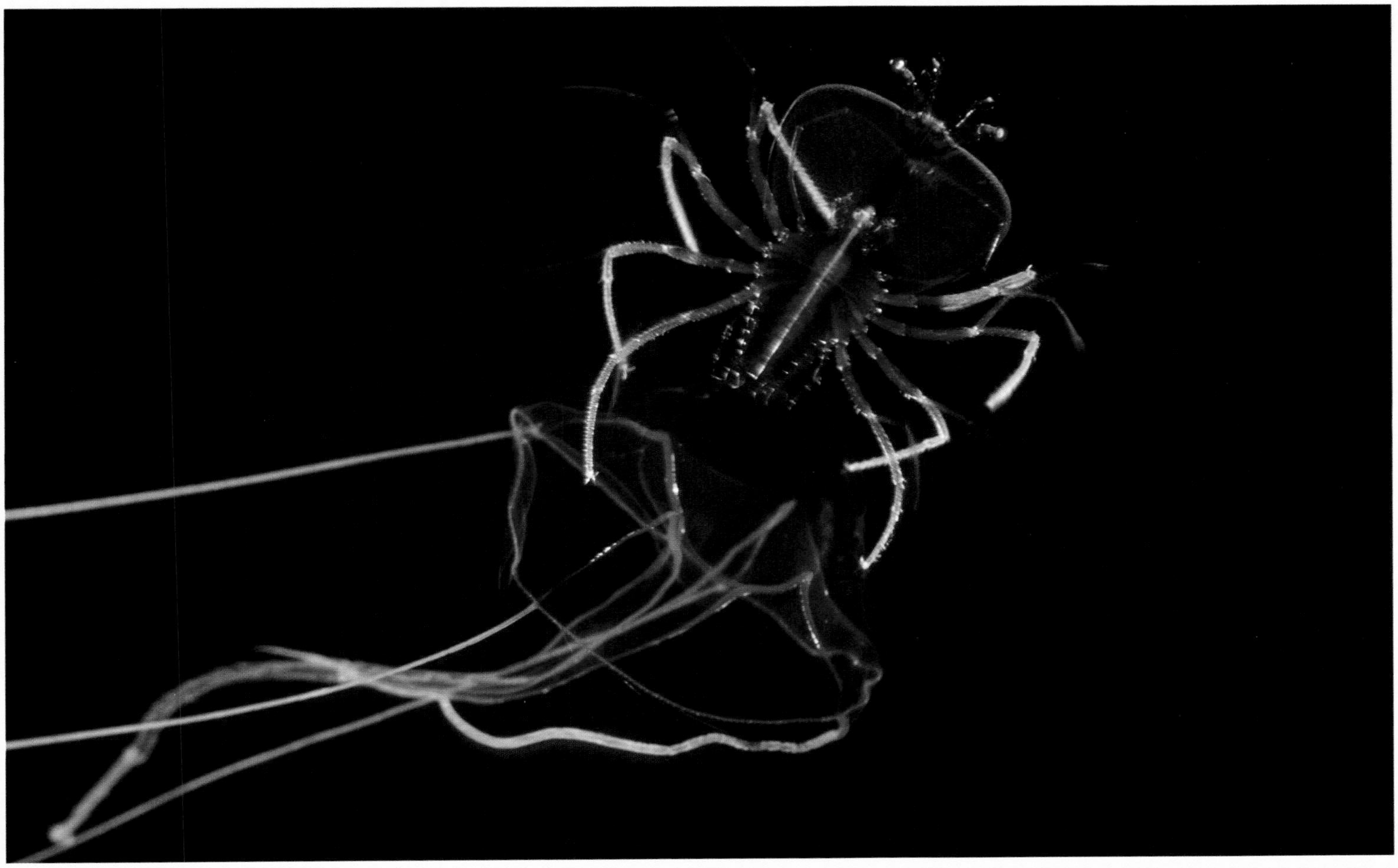

ABOVE 'Hitching a Ride': Offspring of seabed animals spend some time in the plankton; here a larval spiny lobster rides on a sea-jelly in the open ocean, and at the same time, probably gets some protection from predators.

animals. And as there are swimming snails, so there are swimming 'slugs' – snails with no shell: these too are predatory, and devour other animals which they collide with as they float along.

While both the Portuguese man-of-war, *Physalia*, and the by-the-wind-sailor, *Velella*, look something like jellyfish – and indeed belong to the same group – they are in fact more like anemones; but instead of attaching to the rocks of the sea bed, they drift, head-down, on the ocean's surface. The Portuguese man-of-war is probably the best known. Shoals of young *Physalia* look like patches of scum or froth on the water, and these grow into small blue bubbles, sometimes called bluebottles. The adult has a large, gas-filled float, rather like a plastic bag; this may be up to 30cm (12in) long, with a crest acting like a sail. *Velella*, the by-the-wind-sailor, also has a sail across the top, but unlike *Physalia* whose tentacles may extend to several metres, it has only short stubby ones.

In both these surface drifters, the sail is set at an angle to the left or right of the body so it lies at an angle of about 45 degrees to the wind direction. A right-handed animal will be blown south-south-west by a northerly wind, and hence shoals usually contain either right- or left-handed animals; it is also a fact that the northern hemisphere animals are mostly right-handed, and the southern animals are mostly left-handed. Essentially this means that the clockwise wind systems of the north Atlantic and Pacific oceans disperse right-handed animals outwards, so they don't congregate in the centre where food is not so plentiful. The anti-clockwise winds in the southern hemisphere disperse the left-handed animals outwards with the same effect. However, this separation of left- and right-handed animals between the two hemispheres is not a fixed rule, as variations in currents and wind direction cause both types to drift across the equator.

Physalia is in fact a colony of animals that behaves in the same way as a bee swarm, in that every member of the colony is so dependent on every other member that the whole colony acts as one animal. Each colony member or person has a job: one is the float, some are the stinging persons, others are the gastric persons, and yet others the reproductive persons, and all these individuals combine to produce one of the most amazing creatures in the oceans. The float can be filled or topped up by a gas gland, and the creature purposely capsizes its float every five minutes or so to keep its surface moist. The stinging tentacles can extend to 15m (50ft) in length, although some reports claim they can be nearer 60m (200ft); these same

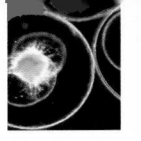

tentacles can inflict a sting that can incapacitate a man for some days.

Deadly though the man-of-war's sting may be, a small fish, *Nomeus*, lives among the tentacles – rather like the famous clown fish living among the tentacles of anemones. The fish do not appear to be stung. Furthermore some specialized predators such as the sunfish, *Mola*, can eat *Physalia*; and in the Mediterranean there is an amazing octopus called *Tremoctopus* that specializes in taking segments of the still-potent stinging tentacles from *Physalia* and then holding these in its suckers so as to make use of the remaining stings for its own ends.

Although *Physalia* belongs to a group called the siphonophores, most of which live beneath the surface, it is

OPPOSITE The Portuguese man-of-war and the by-the-wind-sailor have a sail set at an angle of 45 degrees. The body acts like a drogue so the animal sails across the wind rather than running before it. Why this is so remains conjecture, but having angled sails prevents the animals crowding into one area, as the wind tends to disperse them.

BELOW The violet bubble-raft snail, *Janthina* lives suspended upside down from a raft of bubbles, which it is constantly forming using its foot, and without which the snail would sink. *Janthina* feeds on other floating animals like the Portuguese man-of-war, exuding a slime that seems to render it immune to the stings.

BELOW RIGHT *Pyrosoma* is a sea squirt colony from tropical and subtropical seas. The individuals form a sausage-like tube and each sucks water in from the outside and pumps it out through the centre of the tube so the colony is propelled forward. Some colonies can be 50cm (almost 2ft) or more in length.

adapted to living on the surface of the oceans. *Siphonophores* are amongst the most beautiful and strange creatures, delicate to look at, resembling an exotic water lily, with a float with swimming bells and tentacles. One example is *Physophora*, another *Agalma*.

Seasquirts and Skaters

Sometimes completely unrelated life forms look similar, as they must cope with the same conditions. Sea squirts look and feel like simple jellyfish but actually they are quite complex. The animals live in a skin like a bag with two openings, one to let water in, and the other to squirt it out. Many grow on rocks or harbour walls, but some swim and have been found as deep as 2,000m (6,600ft). The openings in attached sea squirts point up, but the swimming species, or salps, have the inlet at the front and the outlet at the rear so they move through the water by jet propulsion. In the ocean there are some large salps, like *Ctethis*, which can grow to 10 – 15cm (4 – 6in) in length. But even smaller species with individuals less than a centimetre long, can appear much larger as they form colonies that can be as large as half a metre (almost 2ft) or more.

These animals may look like insignificant lumps of jelly, but actually they are distant relatives because they have a simple 'backbone' putting them between animals without a backbone – invertebrates, and those, like us, with – the vertebrates.

One animal group found everywhere on land are the insects, but there is only one ocean insect – the ocean skater, *Halobates*. Ocean skaters are found world-wide in most tropical waters, some close to shore, others miles from land. Like the freshwater pond skater, they walk on the surface film of the water and are carnivorous. Coastal skaters attach their eggs to corals or seaweeds; those in the ocean attach them to drifting debris.

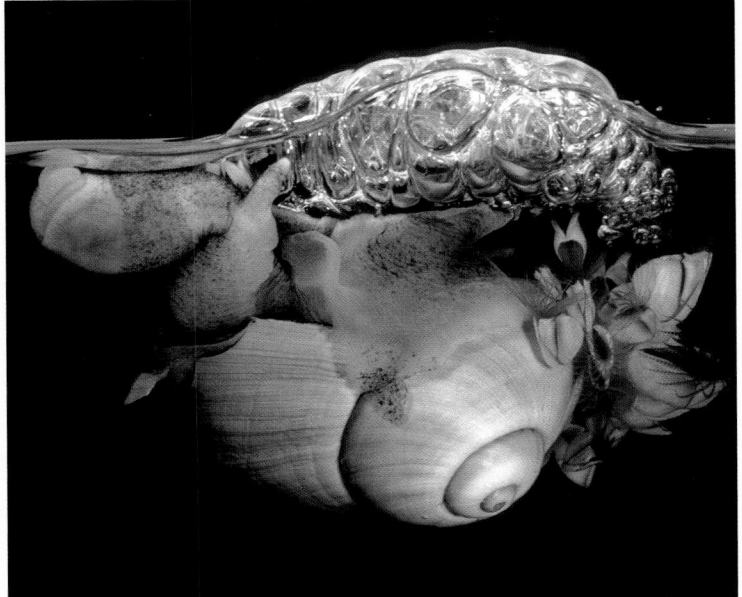

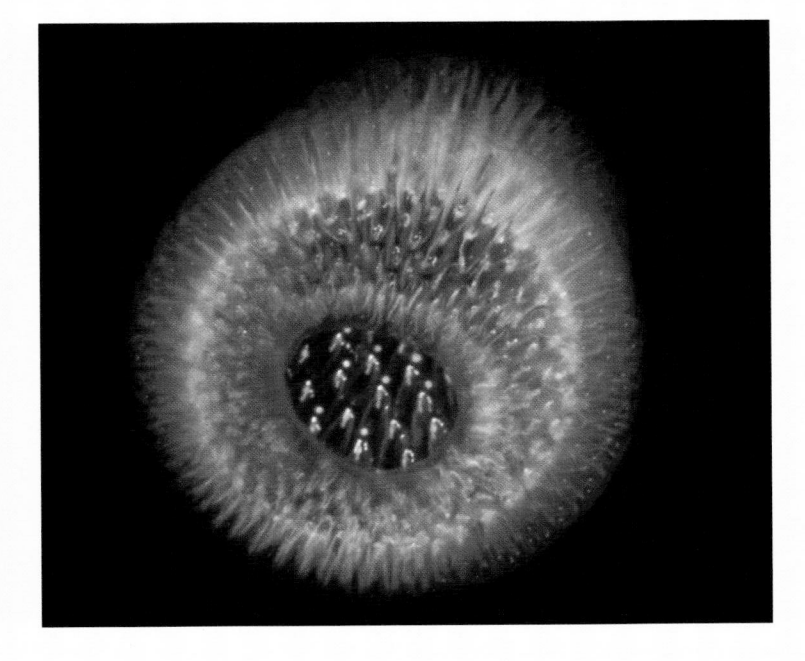

CHAPTER TWO

OCEAN WANDERERS

Some animals undertake great migrations across the oceans, often covering thousands of miles each year. Animals may travel in groups or individually, generally using the same routes each year from generation to generation, congregating for breeding and then spreading out over a wide feeding area. Thus land animals cross mountains, rivers, and vast tracts of land; birds, bats, and insects fly long distances, sometimes crossing entire continents or oceans. Some oceanic animals frequently migrate half way across the world, moving north and south, east and west.

'Summer' and 'winter' apply to the warmest and coldest times of the year, remembering that the seasons are reversed in the northern and southern hemispheres. Consequently, northern and southern hemisphere migrating populations like the whales, probably never meet since those in the north travel towards their breeding grounds in tropical waters at the same time as those in the south are heading for the polar feeding grounds and vice versa.

The blue shark is probably the most travelled of all sharks, wandering throughout the North Atlantic Ocean and often migrating distances of 2,000km to over 3,000 km (1,240 miles to over 1,860 miles).

Why Migrate?

Animals migrate so as to be in the best place for particular periods in their life cycles. They seek food, a good place to mate, and a safe place to bear young, the latter being especially important if the adult is not going to be around to help the growing offspring.

Thus many fish that spend the majority of their lives at sea will move closer inshore to shallow waters and estuaries to spawn because these waters will make better nurseries for their young.

Although most animals do undertake some form of migration during their lives, here we shall look at some of the more spectacular feats of the trans-oceanic travellers. Migration usually corresponds with seasonal changes, and many animals, such as the great whales, travel to the polar and sub-polar regions during the summer months because the long summer days in these areas ensure a good food supply. The onset of shorter days, dwindling food supplies and colder weather is the signal for animals to begin their journeys to find better

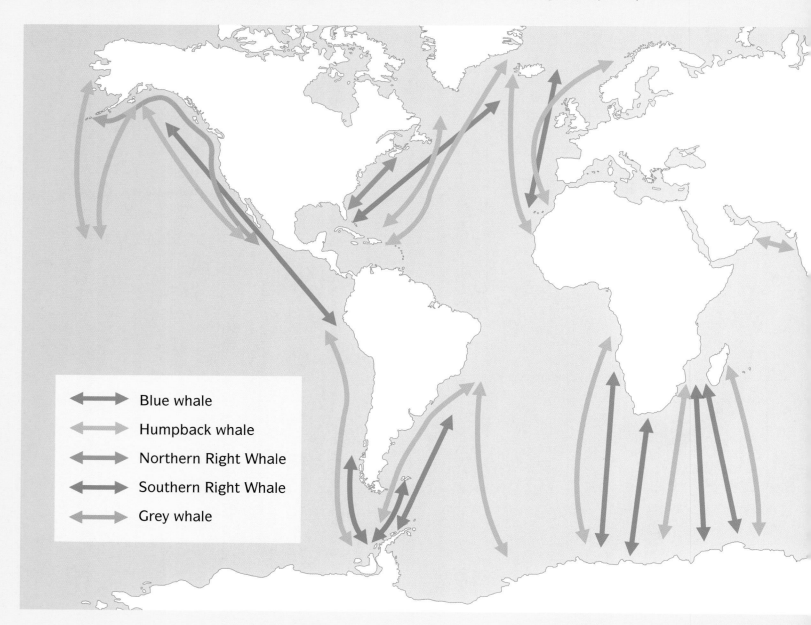

Blue whale

Humpback whale

Northern Right Whale

Southern Right Whale

Grey whale

conditions. While some, such as the great whales, migrate annually with an outward and a homeward journey made in a single year, others take several years to complete their migratory cycles – and some, such as the Pacific salmon, take a whole lifetime.

Navigation

Much work has been done to try to understand how both land and marine animals orientate themselves and migrate across huge distances, but there remain many mysteries.

It is believed that migratory birds use the stars, sun and geographic features as guides, as well as possibly the direction of the earth's magnetic field. Most migratory birds travel within broad north—south air routes known as flyways, the longest journey being made by the Arctic Tern, which migrates between the Arctic and the Antarctic.

In the sea, the stars and geographic features are probably less important than, say, a sense of smell or the ability to use sounds as a form of echolocation. Salmon, for instance, depend on their sense of smell to find their stream of origin, while whales and seals use echolocation to navigate. Some whales also appear to take visual bearings on objects on the shore in their migrations.

LEFT Whale migrations are timed to coincide with the abundant food supplies found during the short summers of the polar regions, when there are massive blooms or growths of food such as krill, or small fish such as herring or capelin.

BELOW Blue whales are the largest animals alive today, and the largest animal ever to have lived; they are bigger than any of the prehistoric dinosaurs. They grow to 30m (100ft) in length, and weigh up to 100,000kg (220,000lb). A new-born blue whale is about 7m (23ft) long and weighs over 2,000kg (4,400lb) – a weight that will double in the first week after birth.

Whale Migrations

The great or baleen (whalebone) whales are probably the most well known oceanic migratory animals, though not all undertake large migrations. The Blue, Grey and Humpback whales have probably been studied the most.

The key motivation for whale migration is to ensure the best conditions for mating and breeding. For most mammals the gestation period, or pregnancy, roughly corresponds to the offspring's size. Horses carry their young for 11 months, rhinoceros for 18 months and elephants for 22 months. But while baleen whale calves are the largest in the world, none have a gestation period longer than 12 months. Apart from needing food, whale calves must fend for themselves from their first breath and so are born with open eyes, alert senses and the ability to follow their mothers immediately.

The relatively short pregnancy and rapid development in the womb requires significant energy output from the mother, which she obtains from abundant supplies of planktonic food. However, the supplies of concentrated planktonic food are intermittent, blooming roughly once every 12 months. So those periods such as giving birth, lactation and weaning, when the greatest demands are being made on the mother, all happen in the places and at the times where food supplies are most abundant.

Despite the size of whales, little was known about their migration habits until scientists developed satellite-tracking technologies. This has shown that the animals can move around the oceans at speeds much faster than previously believed. One blue whale migrated more than 16,000km (10,000 miles) in 10 months. The animals appear to be moving from one fertile zone to another and some whales have now been seen to cover over 225,000km (140,000 miles) in the span of months. But many mysteries still remain; for example, a mother Blue Whale tagged in the Sea of Cortez during the winter never returned to California during the summer as expected, staying with her calf instead.

The Baleen Whales

An animal the size of the big baleen whale is successful because of the existence of large quantities of planktonic food; but because these supplies are not present year-round, events in the life of a great whale that require increased energy levels only occur when food is at its most plentiful.

LEFT Humpbacks can swim at 5 knots, but on long journeys they travel slower, often resting and socialising. Summer in the north Atlantic finds humpbacks feeding on small fish like capelin between the Gulf of Maine and Iceland, having migrated up from the West Indies along the eastern seaboard of the US. They use a system of 'bubble netting' which concentrates the fish into shoals, then with their mouths agape they lunge upwards through the shoal to catch the fish.

ABOVE The migration of the California grey whale is perhaps the best documented of all whales, probably because of the close proximity to the west coast of North America where they follow a north-south route regularly each year.

Eight of the 10 baleen whales have gestation periods between 10 and 12 months, and all spend the season of plenty in polar waters, concentrating largely on feeding and returning fat and well fed to warmer waters for mating. Pregnant females are once again in peak condition when they return to tropical breeding grounds a year later to give birth and start nursing. The time when calves rely on milk, or the lactation period, is roughly six months, which means that calves are weaned by the time they reach the feeding grounds where they can eat as much as they need. A large baleen whale produces as much as 600 litres (132 gallons) of milk a day, and the calves can double their weight in the first week.

The period of gestation of the other species of baleen whales, the rare pygmy right whale and the more common tropical whale, is unknown. Both, however, live in tropical waters, and it is possible that their life histories are not as tightly tied to the annual peaks dictated by polar plankton.

The Blue Whale

Most blue whales follow the classic migration pattern, travelling thousands of kilometres annually. They move between winter breeding grounds in warmer, low latitude waters around the tropics where they mate and give birth, and summer feeding grounds in the cooler, high latitude waters of either the Arctic or the Antarctic. Here they feed for three to four months on the rich supply of krill and other food that occurs in huge numbers in polar waters. They then migrate back to the tropics, segregated by sex and age, the older and pregnant whales migrating first, with the sexually immature whales bringing up the rear. Generally the larger, older whales migrate the furthest north or south.

During this migration it is thought that Blue whales eat virtually nothing for at least four months, surviving on body reserves, although some recent satellite tracking data appears to indicate that the whales can move rapidly from one feeding ground to another and hence may actually feed all year. The calves are suckled for seven months, and then follow their mothers on the spring migration towards the polar seas. Once weaned, the calves feed on krill and follow the normal migration cycle.

The Grey Whale

California grey whales migrate along the west coast of North America. They move south from Alaska in early winter to breed in the warm, shallow lagoons along the Mexican coast. The most popular breeding lagoons are San Ignacio Lagoon, Scammon's Lagoon, and Magdalena Bay, on the Pacific coast of Baja California, Mexico. Then, around February, they migrate north to feed in the Arctic waters of the western

Beaufort and Bering Seas, northwest of Alaska. A few, mainly younger, whales make a shorter journey north from Mexico, stopping off along the coastline stretching between northern California, Oregon, Washington State, USA, and British Columbia, Canada. The whales feed in all parts of their range, and Greys are present all year round near Vancouver Island off the west coast of Canada.

The California Grey has a close relative on the other side of the Pacific, which is the Asian or West Pacific Grey Whale. There are very few of these animals remaining, but the tiny population migrates north from winter calving grounds off the Korean Peninsula and Japan, to summer feeding grounds in the northern Okhotsk Sea off the Russian Far East coast, particularly around Sakhalin Island.

The Humpback Whale

Most humpback whales make mammoth journeys every year between their feeding and breeding sites. They are capable of travelling at five knots, but during long journeys they average about a knot or so, often resting and socializing along the way. However, not all members of a particular population will travel together: for example, the humpbacks that pass the eastern shores of Australia on their way to summer feeding grounds in Antarctica each year, stop off in the warm waters of Hervey Bay. The first to arrive there are groups of older juveniles, followed by mature males and then by mothers and calves.

Other humpbacks on the east side of the Atlantic are found off the coast of Norway during the summer months, and during the winter off West Africa and the Cape Verde Islands. Pacific humpback whales feed in the area of the northern Pacific Rim, along the coasts of eastern Russia in the west, and Alaska in the east. Then during the winter months, humpbacks in the North Pacific breed around some of Japan's southern islands, the Hawaiian Islands and along Mexico's western coast. However, there is a population of humpbacks in the Arabian Sea that appears not to migrate, perhaps because the warm waters are not only suitable for breeding, but also rich enough in food all year round.

South of the equator during the northern summer, humpbacks are found feeding in the southern ocean around Antarctica. The populations travel towards the equator and spend the winter months in breeding grounds off Brazil, off the

RIGHT The migrations of Right Whales are not as long as the blue, humpback and grey whales, but both the Northern and Southern Right Whales follow similar routes, although they prefer to stay in the cooler, higher latitudes.

OPPOSITE Sperm whales have a longer pregnancy lasting up to 15 months and the young take milk for a year before weaning. The calves are born just after adult males leave the tropical breeding grounds so the harem, gathered for breeding, reverts to being a nursery.

west coast of Africa between Mozambique and Madagascar, and off northeast and northwest Australia. They can be seen feeding on large shoals of krill off the coast of Eden in New South Wales, and are also found around some of the South Pacific Islands such as Tonga and New Caledonia. The Southeast Pacific humpback whale breeds mainly along the coasts of Colombia, Ecuador and Panama, with a northern limit around Costa Rica.

The Right Whales

Right whales are so called because they swim slowly, and they float when they're killed, which made them the 'right' whales to hunt in the early whaling days. These whales are found around the Arctic throughout the year, and formed the basis of the eighteenth-century whaling expeditions. One description of these whales by perhaps the first whale expert, William Scoresby (also a successful whaling captain) in 1820, states that the head '...may, when the mouth is open, present a cavity capable of containing a ship's jolly boat full of men, being 6 or 8 feet wide [1.8–2.4m], 10 or 12 feet high [3–3.6m] and 15 or 16 feet long [4.5–4.8m]'. The baleen, or whalebone, is 3 – 3.5 metres (10 – 12ft) long in the centre of the upper jaw. During the winter and spring, southern rights are found in their coastal mating and calving grounds, which lie mainly along the southern coasts of Africa (Hermanus, South Africa is a particularly good place to see them), South America (around Chile and Argentina – Peninsula Valdes is a well known

habitat) and in the Great Australian Bight, as well as along the western coast of New Zealand. During summer they migrate to colder, food-rich waters near Antarctica, but precisely where is not known. Most appear to stay in the mid-Southern ocean, but some do feed at the edge of the pack ice.

Some northern right whales make annual migrations between winter breeding and calving grounds in the waters of the European coast and Norwegian Sea, even as far south as the Caribbean and the Canary Isles. In the Pacific they can be seen in a broad arc between the Sea of Japan, through the Aleutian Islands and down the coast of California. Most females give birth in the coastal waters of southeast USA, off the states of Florida and Georgia; however, males and non-calving females are rarely seen in this area, and their whereabouts during the winter is not known. In the spring, aggregations of northern rights can be seen in the Great South Channel, east of Cape Cod, and in Massachusetts Bay as they travel north to their summer grounds.

The Sperm Whales

Another large whale that has teeth and not baleen is the sperm whale. The males spend their summers in rich polar waters, but the females remain in the lower latitudes. Lactation continues for over a year, which may ensure that females do not ovulate and become impregnated with the first return of the breeding bulls, and can devote their full attention to the care and protection of the growing young.

Turtles

Turtles comprise one of only three groups of reptiles that live in the sea, and they are also great wanderers of the oceans. The other reptile groups are sea snakes and a species of lizard, the marine iguana, that lives on and around the Galapagos Islands.

There are several different species of turtle, and some have different races in the Atlantic and Pacific oceans separated by the land mass of the Americas. The green turtle, *Chelonia mydas*, is possibly the best known, but other shelled turtles include the loggerhead, the hawksbill and the ridley turtle, the latter being the smallest with a carapace length of around 65cm (26in) and weighing less than 45kg (100lb).

Being reptiles, turtles are cold-blooded which means that their internal body temperature is similar to the outside – hence they live in the tropical and sub tropical areas of the world's oceans. Leatherbacks, on the other hand, are not uncommon in the cooler waters of the North Atlantic off the west coast of the British Isles and the eastern seaboard of Canada. At first sight this is unusual for cold-blooded animals, but leatherbacks can keep their core body temperature warmer than the surrounding water, which allows them to flourish in ocean regions where other marine reptiles cannot. In the early 1980s, it was estimated that 115,000 adult female leatherbacks existed worldwide, roughly half of them thought to be nesting in western Mexico. Unfortunately, recent years have seen an alarming decline in the number of nesting leatherbacks.

Early Life

Like all reptiles, turtles start life as an egg. The females bury their eggs about 60cm (24in) down in a sandy pit above high water on a tropical beach. After hatching, the young turtle, along with its hundred or so brothers and sisters, pushes upwards to lie just below the surface of the sand, waiting for nightfall; then they push out of the nest and waddle to the sea. But from here the young turtle seems to 'disappear'.

The next few years are spent wandering the oceans, in some cases for thousands of miles. Not much is known about this period in the turtle's life, which is, therefore, often referred to as 'the lost years'. Hatchling green turtles, once they leave the beach, appear to move into what are known as 'convergence zones' – areas of down-welling currents – in the open ocean: this is known as the pelagic, or 'open-ocean' phase. Here they grow until they reach about 20 – 25cm (8 – 10in) long, feeding

on drifting plants and animals, including jellyfish and the Portuguese man-of-war. When they reach shallow areas they become herbivorous, feeding on sea grasses and seaweeds. They are often found foraging over coral reefs, worm reefs and rocky bottoms, using the reefs or rocky outcrops near feeding pastures as resting areas, both at night and during the day. It can take around 17 years for green turtles to grow from about 30cm to 75cm (12 – 30in).

The major nesting colonies of Atlantic green turtles are located on Ascension Island, Aves Island, Costa Rica, Suriname, the United States Virgin Islands, Puerto Rico and in Florida.

Turtles usually return to nest on the beach where they were hatched, and many also return to the same foraging areas. But although the navigation feats of the green turtle are well known, they are not well understood. Hatchlings and adult females on the nesting beach orientate towards the ocean by following the light, which is usually brighter from the sea than from land (assuming that no hotels or tourist resorts have been built at the top of the beach!); but how the animals navigate in

LEFT Perhaps the best known, and also the largest hard-shelled turtle, is the green turtle, *Chelonia mydas*. The adult's shell, or carapace, can grow to a metre (3ft) long, and the animals weigh around 150kg (330lb).

OPPOSITE The leatherback turtle, *Dermochelys coriacea*, is the largest turtle and does not have a hard shell: its carapace is flexible and has a rubbery texture, and is shaped somewhat like a barrel. This turtle has extremely long front flippers, and adults can reach over 2.5m (8ft) in length. The largest leatherback on record was a male stranded on the west coast of Wales in the British Isles in 1988: he weighed 916kg (2,035lb).

the open sea between foraging grounds or to nesting beaches remains largely a mystery, although it has been suggested that they may somehow be able to use the earth's magnetic field. It is all the more wondrous when you consider that young turtles have no parents to guide them and show the way.

Green turtles feed in marine pastures in quiet, low wave-energy areas, but nest on high wave-energy beaches, and hence their feeding and nesting habitats are located some distance apart. Green turtles that nest on Ascension Island forage along the coast of Brazil, some 1,000km (620 miles) away! But the location of the foraging grounds of other green turtles, such as those that nest in Florida, remains unknown.

Breeding

After a number of years spent in the oceans and foraging, the turtles return to the shore to breed. Green turtles reach sexual maturity at any time between 20 to 50 years, though the age for other species can vary.

The turtles dig their nests at the top of sandy beaches and lay an average clutch of 110 – 115 eggs, but the female will return to the beach most evenings over a period of about three weeks until she has laid about 1,000 eggs. Some nights she may not be successful; either the sand crumbles, filling the hole, or there may be obstructions caused by roots, or rocks, but she will continue until her task is complete. Having done so, she returns to the sea, and wanders the oceans for the next two or three years before returning to breed again at the same beach.

The temperature at which the eggs are incubated determines the sex of hatchling turtles. Eggs incubated below a pivotal temperature, which varies among populations, mainly produce males, and eggs incubated above this temperature mainly result in females.

Ocean Wanderers

RIGHT Adult green turtles mate just offshore. Little is known about the males, but they must also migrate to the nesting beaches each year, though evidently do not emerge from the sea. They have especially enlarged claws on the front flippers used for clasping the female's shell during mating. Then the female, like her mother did years previously, emerges from the sea at night and pushes her way up the beach above the high-water mark, where she digs a hole and lays a clutch of about a hundred eggs. Egg laying takes an average of about two hours. After covering the eggs and spreading loose sand over the nest, the female will sometimes go further and dig another 'nest', but without laying eggs. This false nest is clearly to lead any predators away. Then, excreting salt in tears from her eyes, she pushes herself back to the sea.

BELOW & OPPOSITE Turtle hatchlings are 5 – 10cm (2 – 4in) long, depending on the species, and weigh about 25g (1oz). Once hatched they wait for nightfall, and then, under cover of darkness, they scramble out and make for the safety of the sea, running the gauntlet between hungry ghost crabs and seabirds until they reach the water. The young turtle is well camouflaged: from above its back is dark to match the sea, and from below, the underside is light to blend with the sky.

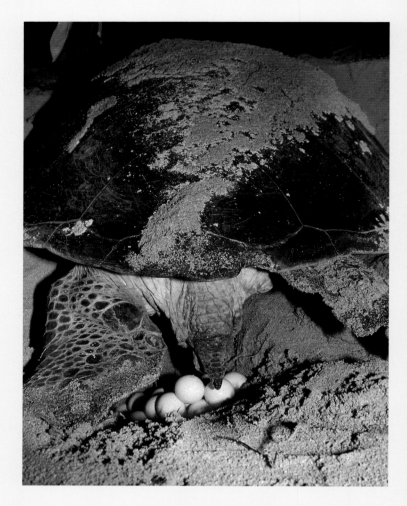

BELOW After a period in the open sea eating mainly jellyfish, turtles find foraging areas in shallower waters, mostly eating sea grasses and seaweeds. This hawksbill turtle is eating soft coral from a Red Sea coral reef; filamentous matter from the coral can be seen around the turtle's head.

Living Dangerously

The turtle's life, particularly in its early years, is precarious as they succumb to large predators and, unfortunately, to the pollution created by human society. Even adults face danger – most commonly from human activities. Hunting has already caused the extinction of some populations, as has the destruction and loss of nesting and foraging sites, from the expansion of tourism. Entanglement in fishing gear, such as shrimp nets, and pollution exact a heavy toll on turtle populations the world over. Despite measures to protect the animals, like the use of special turtle exclusion devices in shrimp nets, the survival of all marine turtle species remains in the balance with the acknowledgement that they are 'endangered'.

Fish

Many fish, too, achieve spectacular feats of oceanic migration. Some have lives that span both the freshwater and ocean worlds, the best known for this perhaps being the salmon.

Both the Atlantic and Pacific salmon are spawned in the headwaters of rivers during late autumn or winter; here they remain until they are young adults, when they move downstream and out to sea to join their elders. The salmon spawns in clean water over a gravel bed, and the young feed on the egg yolk until it is all used up, by which time they are big enough to hunt for other food.

For Pacific salmon, spawning is their last act as the spent animals subsequently die, but the spent and exhausted female Atlantic salmon returns to the sea, though males may stay in fresh water until the end of the spawning season. The young fish (smolt and parr) spend between one and four years in fresh water before making their way down to the sea, where they remain for at least a year. The older male parr may become sexually mature before entering the sea, and often fertilize the eggs of the adult females. The adult fish spend from 5–18 months feeding on a variety of animals, especially small fish and crustaceans in the sea, before returning to spawn.

Across the Atlantic

The common eel achieves a feat of migration that is just as remarkable. It is found in European lakes and rivers where it spends most of its life – but to breed, these eels leave the relative comfort and safety of their rivers and lakes to swim to the coast, after which there is little further direct knowledge of their movements until their eggs are found in the deep waters of the Sargasso Sea, the area just north of the Tropic of Cancer on the western side of the Atlantic ocean.

In other words, the adults have swum, against the prevailing currents, almost all the way across the Atlantic ocean. The young are transparent and shaped like a knife-blade, and they gradually drift back across the Atlantic Ocean to Europe and North Africa on the prevailing current, a journey that takes two or three years. When they reach the coastal waters they assume the normal yellow-brown colour of the young eel (elver). When they are about 5 – 10cm (2 – 4in) long they make their way up the rivers, or sometimes settle in coastal waters.

Warm Waters

Other fish, such as the albacore and the skipjack and blue-fin tunas, are found in all warm seas. Although fish are generally cold-blooded, these species often maintain an internal body temperature that is higher than the surrounding water.

Tuna, like many other large fish such as hammerheads, also migrate to waters around seamounts. These huge mountains rise almost vertically from the sea bed and cause a disturbance in the current flows, which brings nutrients to the surface. Marine life abounds around these natural features, and they act like a magnet to top predators.

LEFT Salmon can recognize the waters of their birth by their smell. They undertake a gruelling journey to return to the waters where they were spawned to spawn themselves. When they begin this trip they are in prime condition, but they stop eating when they leave the sea and arrive months later, exhausted by their fight upstream against swift currents and over falls. Those that survive the trip spawn. For the Pacific salmon, this is its last act, as they die after spawning, but Atlantic salmon spawn more than once.

ABOVE Tuna in both the Pacific and Atlantic embark on long migrations. The presence of large shoals in particular places are predictable. They cross the Atlantic and in the summer some migrate from the Mediterranean to Norway and the North Sea, but they do not inhabit water colder than 10 – 14°C (50 – 60°F) and are not found in the northern or southern waters during winter. In summer they school near the surface and may come close inshore. In winter they live deeper, sometimes to a depth of 180m (600ft).

BELOW The eels of western Europe and North Africa spend most of their lives in rivers and lakes. But when they are between 7 and 20 years old, and ½ to 1m (2 – 3 ft) long, their eye increases in diameter and becomes specialised for deep ocean vision; their gut reduces in size, their sex cells enlarge and their colour changes from yellow-brown to silver-grey. Then, on a moonless night in autumn, they begin an incredible journey from the rivers to the coast and across the Atlantic, even travelling short distances over land.

Sharks

The blue shark, *Prionace glauca*, is one of the most travelled species of shark. These predators sometimes travel in groups, and have been observed rounding up schools of fish for prey. They have extremely long pectoral fins and a long, pointed snout, and the body is a brilliant dark blue with a white underside. They are found worldwide in tropical and temperate seas, often on the surface. The record distance so far achieved by a shark is held by a blue that swam the 6,919km (4,299 miles) from New York state, where it was released, to Brazil.

Basking sharks live mainly in open water, often in shoals of 50 or 60, but they migrate towards the shore in summer. During the winter they retreat to deeper water to hibernate. Little is known about their breeding habits, but it is thought that they give birth after a pregnancy of up to three-and-a-half years. Basking sharks occur in the North and South Pacific, and the Atlantic and Indian oceans, and were once extensively hunted from the shores of New England, Scotland, Ireland and Norway for the oil in their liver. Until recently, they were still hunted to supply fins for the Japanese market. Fortunately the species is now protected.

CHAPTER THREE

LIVING STRUCTURES: CORAL REEFS AND ATOLLS

A coral reef is an association of ancient life forms that has been in existence for about 200 million years. The Great Barrier reef which stretches along the north east coast of Australia is perhaps the most well known, and is the largest living structure on earth. Corals generally live in clear, warm, shallow water mainly between the Tropics of Cancer and Capricorn, only extending further north and south where there are warm currents. However there are corals found in deeper and colder waters and recently whole deep sea coral forests have been discovered in various parts of the world.

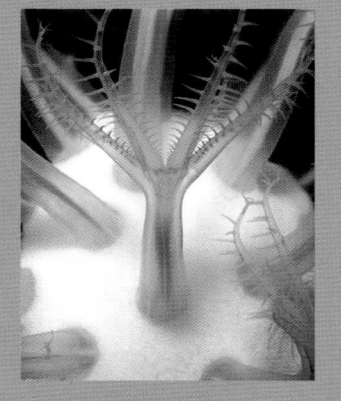

Corals are tiny animals called polyps. They resemble sea anemones with a slit-like mouth opening surrounded by tentacles. Each polyp develops a cup of limestone around itself, produced by cells on its lower sides and bottom, which forms reefs.

A Diverse Marine Ecosystem

Corals are one of the most diverse ecosystems on the planet with over 6,000 different species covering an estimated 300,000 – 600,000 square km (116,000 – 231,000 square miles) and found in the waters of over 100 countries.

Coral polyps divide as they grow and form colonies which build on top of each other to form a reef. Individual colonies may be 1,000 years old and reefs may be many thousands of years old. Living within corals are minute plants called *zooxanthellae* that are the main source of the colours found in a coral reef. Corals feed mainly at night using their tentacles to catch minute life forms in the plankton.

An atoll is formed when an island (usually the tops of volcanoes) that was surrounded by a fringing reef, sank or when the sea level rose, which has happened from time to time. The fringing reefs grew continuously, covering older coral, to keep pace with the changing sea level, eventually forming a circle with a central lagoon – an atoll. Time after

time the coral was exposed and covered until today the original island may be a mile below the reef, buried under layers of coral which is now rock.

Corals occur world-wide but are most abundant in warmer waters. Fringing reefs mainly lie around islands, separated from the shore by narrow, shallow, sandy lagoons. Barrier reefs, on the other hand, grow on the edge of continental shelves, separated from the mainland by deep, wide lagoons. The largest barrier reefs are the Great Barrier Reef in Australia, which is about 2,000km (1,250 miles) long, and the Belize Barrier Reef in the Caribbean.

Corals can reproduce by producing buds or just splitting from the original polyp. But sexual reproduction also occurs;

LEFT The anemone-like polyps can vary in size from as small as a pinhead up to giants of 30cm (12in) in diameter.

ABOVE Most atolls are found in the Pacific where volcanic islands are common, but there are some in the Indian Ocean and a few in the Caribbean. The Maldives, in the Indian Ocean, where the word 'atoll' originated, is a country made up entirely of atolls.

RIGHT Each coral species has its own growth pattern which often gives them some of their common names. This is a brain coral but there are other examples such as staghorn, elkhorn, star coral, mushroom coral, and organ pipe coral.

in some, the eggs are fertilised internally and then brooded inside the parent's body. The young coral larva or planula is released into the sea to be carried by currents as a part of the plankton until it eventually settles on the seabed to form new coral areas. When found on the shore, coral is brittle and white but the holes in which the anemone-like polyps lived can be seen. Living coral is brilliantly coloured and reefs can resemble magnificent underwater gardens.

Moving Coral

A few corals are not attached to the seabed, for example in the mushroom coral, *Fungia*, the young grows into a single stalked individual with a flat disc-shaped top. This coral disc eventually breaks away but continues to grow, carried by water and sand movements as an unattached organism. *Fungia* is able to turn over if accidentally inverted on the sand and individuals can move themselves across the sand. Sometimes the stalk grows new discs of coral that, in turn, can break off to grow independently.

Home to Unknown Numbers

Coral reefs provide a wide range of different habitats, so they contain thousands of different animals. More types of fish are found on reefs than anywhere else in the sea. They range from large sharks to tiny fish, like the gobies and damsel fish. But although the fish may be the most obvious life forms, it is believed that about 90 per cent of all reef animals are small invertebrates yet to be discovered. These, like many of the tiny molluscs, crustaceans, sponges and tubeworms that are already

BELOW A strange territory is occupied by the little clownfish, brilliantly patterned in orange and white, with its unique immunity to the stings of its host sea anemone. It defends its chosen home valiantly against rival clownfish, to whom its flag-like colours announce its ownership. It is possible that the gaudy colour of the fish helps pay for its lodgings, by attracting other small prey fish into the death trap of the anemone's tentacles.

known, will never be seen by divers and snorkellers because they live in caves, cracks and crevices in the coral.

The greatest diversity of reef plants and animals is found in South-east Asia, ranging from the Philippines to the Great Barrier Reef. In this area a single reef may have over 3,000 different kinds of plants and animals. The diversity of life is lower in the Caribbean, as a result of the geological history of this region, yet up to a thousand species may still inhabit the richer reefs.

Coral Reef Fish

Coral reef fish encompass one of the greatest selections of sizes, shapes and colours present in any one area. Many of them, like the angelfish, feed on the coral polyps or sponges and have small mouths but sharp teeth at the front to snatch at their food. Other fish, such as some of the butterflyfish, have long snouts for poking into crevices and cracks or among sea urchin spines to eat small invertebrate animals.

Some butterflyfish have bright false 'eyes' near the tail or on the gill covers to mislead an enemy as to the direction in which the intended prey will flee.

Most of the small to medium sized fish living among corals are flattened sideways so they can swim efficiently among the coral branches and twigs. But the presence of so many fish leads to a huge amount of competition for different places to live, and once a home has been found it will be vigorously defended, even by the smallest of fish. Damselfish, which are a centimetre (⅖ in) or so long, will attack anything which threatens their habitat, even much larger animals, or its own kind; they will even take a nip at divers. Clearly, defending the eggs and young is vital – and once again, the male damselfish will stand guard, hovering over a clutch of eggs.

Bright colours, which normally act to keep fish well spaced out must change at times to allow mating to take place between two fish that would otherwise be hostile. For example, boldly marked black and white damselfish turn a dull grey while mating and spawning. It is quite common for young fish to be more highly coloured than sexually mature adults. The only time two fish with the same gaudy colours live harmoniously together is in a permanently mated pair, such as

OPPOSITE A vast number of animals and plants inhabit coral reefs, which makes them second only to rainforests in species richness. This huge diversity is a result of careful sharing of a reef by all its inhabitants. Tubeworms are cemented to the coral; the worm's head, with tentacles to catch prey, and gills protrude from the tube. There are numerous anemones that use stings on their tentacles to catch food such as small fish and shrimps. But one anemone has a fish which lives unharmed among its tentacles and is even camouflaged to resemble the anemone.

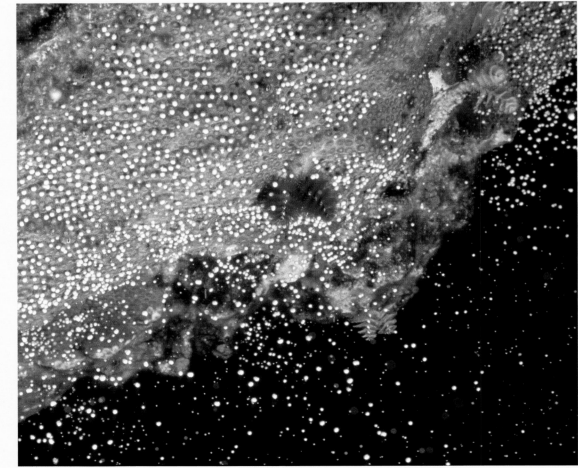

LEFT Some corals shed their eggs and sperm into the water where fertilisation occurs. To ensure the best odds of enough eggs being fertilised, many corals spawn together on one night of the year – a spectacular event that turns the sea milky. Like the Palolo worms in chapter 1, the timing of this spawning depends on the phase of the moon and happens 5 days after the full moon in October/November.

occurs with the blue angelfish or the Beau Gregory (a type of damselfish). These pairs chase other fish from their territory even more fiercely than a single fish does.

Coral-like Camouflage

Bigger fish will try to eat smaller fish, and so the smaller fish will try their best to escape. Again, the large number of different species has led to reef fish evolving colours and patterns that either camouflage themselves or attempt to ward off prey. For example, having false 'eyes' on their flanks or tails makes them look like a much larger fish than they actually are. Poisonous spines, fins or the ability to swell to a larger size are all techniques that have been adopted to ensure survival.

A Symbiotic Relationship

One fish has a home no other fish would like and gets protection from it: the clown fish or anemone fish is famous for living among a sea anemone's tentacles, which would be lethal for other small fish. There are about 28 different clown fish species found on reefs in the Indo-Pacific and some places like the Maldives, Seychelles, Oman and Madagascar even have their own particular species. The relationship between anemone and clown fish appears to be very personal because if introduced to a new anemone in a tank, the fish behaves as if it is being stung. When returned to its original anemone the fish performs an elaborate 'dance' among the tentacles: little by little allowing the tentacles to touch its fins, then the rest of its body, until it appears to be immunised against the sting.

The fish's immunity derives from a covering of mucus and during its 'dance', the mucus is spread onto the anemone's tentacles, and mucus from the tentacles is spread over the fish. How this actually works is not really understood.

But what benefit does the anemone get when it can survive happily without its lodger? This is open to conjecture, but, as anemones are permanently attached, they need to rely on food brought to them in the currents or accidentally found in the case of an unwary shrimp or fish. With a clown fish in residence extra food is provided as the fish makes short forays onto the surrounding reef to bring food back to the anemone. The fish may also act as a cleaner, ensuring the anemone does not get smothered.

The common clownfish is perhaps the most well known. A pair will spawn on a cleaned piece of coral or rock next to the anemone and both parents share guarding the eggs. After hatching, the young spend about two weeks floating in the sea before heading back to the reef to look for an anemone host. Once found, the fish aggressively defends 'their' anemone, which also protects the anemone from would-be predators.

Many small fish living in and around coral reefs constantly do battle not just with prey and predators, but also with their own kind. This is sometimes violent, as they are oblivious to danger when enraged. This aggressive territorial behaviour ensures that individuals are well spaced out. Most aggression is shown by threat displays and sparring rather than serious fighting and, once established in its territory, a fish is normally able to drive away all rivals without actually joining in combat.

RIGHT Fish living on coral reefs have evolved specialized ways of using different habitats and food; for instance, the butterflyfish has a long pointed snout that it can poke into small cracks to search for food. Some have false 'eyes' on the tail to distract potential predators

ABOVE Parrotfish have sharp teeth for rasping small algae that grow on coral and rocks. They are an efficient recycling machine as the rasping turns the coral into fine sand.

LEFT Cracks and crevices are good hiding places. Trigger fish can wedge themselves in to tight spaces by using their 'trigger' (a spine or series of spines in front of the dorsal fin). They jam their trigger up into the roof of a crevice and pull themselves into the hiding space. Triggerfish also crunch coral, creating a noise which seems to be either a territorial signal or directs others to food sources.

Corals in Cooler Waters

The spectacular coral reefs and atolls of warm, clear waters are not, however, the only ones in existence: in the cooler, temperate waters of the world are solitary corals or cup corals, perhaps rather less spectacular, but still a wonder.

Like their tropical relatives, cup coral polyps make hard limestone cases and grow attached to underwater cliffs and rocks, yet unlike warm water corals they do not form reefs, but grow as single penny-sized individuals.

Also found in cooler waters are soft corals. These don't have the hard limestone case but instead their body is more flexible, somewhat like rubber. The polyps grow in colonies and, like cup corals, are found on rocky faces underwater. They are commonly called dead man's fingers.

Deep Ocean Corals

Scientists have long known about corals in shallow tropical waters, and the soft corals of temperate shallow areas; deep-sea corals were discovered in the 1800s. But it was recently discovered that coral forests are widespread in certain cold and deep ocean habitats, many centred along the edges of continental shelves. Whole deep-sea coral fields have now been discovered in Japan, Tasmania, New Zealand, Alaska, British Columbia, California, Nova Scotia, Maine, North Carolina, Florida, Colombia, Brazil, Norway, Sweden, UK, Ireland and Mauritania. There could be more species of corals in cold and deep ocean waters than in tropical shallows.

However, deep water coral reefs do share one similarity with their tropical cousins which is that they provide a habitat for other animals such as lobsters and other crustaceans, shellfish, starfish and brittlestars, sea urchins and many fish including redfish, saithe, cod and ling. A wide variety of animals grow on the coral itself, including sponges, bryozoans or sea mats, and hydroids or sea firs.

Many deep water corals, such as sea-trees or black corals, grow long fragile branches as they are undisturbed by the turbulence of storms on the surface, although many fine branches are able to make use of deep sea currents to bring food.

A Slow Grower

Lophelia is one relatively recent discovery. Unlike its tropical relatives, this coral does not need algae and light for survival and it is mainly found in depths of 200 – 1,000m (650 – 3,280ft). The record for the deepest coral reef is 3,000m (9,800ft), although they can be found in shallower water up to about 40m (131ft). Also unlike its tropical relatives, it prefers water temperatures of 4 – 12°C (39 – 53°F) and is found world-wide, though not in polar regions.

Deep-water corals grow very slowly. *Lophelia* reefs grow at about 1 millimetre a year. When considering that the highest reefs found so far are 35m (114ft) high on the Sula Ridge off Norway, simple arithmetic can tell you that this reef is old. Fragments taken from this reef have been dated at eight and half thousand years, which is just after the end of the last Ice Age.

ABOVE Cold-water corals, like this black coral, live in cool, temperate waters. In the deep sea, there are extensive coral-reef systems that are many hundreds of years old.

OPPOSITE Soft corals and cup corals grow on rocks and underwater cliffs in cooler temperate waters. Soft corals, like these dead man's fingers, don't have a limestone case.

Threats to Corals

In shallow waters, coral reefs are frequently disturbed by natural events. Hurricanes and tropical storms can reduce reefs to rubble, and corals are often affected by diseases such as black-band disease, which spreads over whole colonies, progressively killing the polyps.

The crown-of-thorns starfish is another coral killer. It feeds voraciously on corals, and if present in large numbers, can reduce a reef to a mass of dead coral skeletons in just a few weeks.

Warm-water tropical corals need clear water to grow, and anything that affects the clarity of the water, such as discharges of sewage or other pollution, can have a severe effect. As corals are attached animals, they are in constant danger of being buried by sediment, and so they have a covering of hairs or cilia all over their exposed bodies, especially around the mouth, which are constantly sweeping away material that might smother them. But changes in land use, such as forest clearance and intensification of agriculture, cause increased erosion: soil is washed into rivers and out to sea, silting up reefs along the coast, and the water becomes murky and stops sunlight, vital for coral growth, reaching the reef. If sediment settles on top of corals, it may smother them. This can also happen during the dredging of channels and harbours.

Sensitive Creatures

Corals are also very sensitive to water temperatures, and global climate change is causing a significant increase in water temperatures, which has killed huge areas of coral reef, a phenomenon known as bleaching. If the bleaching is not too severe, they can recover, but if it is repeated, this results in a massive loss of coral reefs. As the oceans warm up due to global climate change, corals may experience increasing difficulty in recovering from bleaching episodes. In fact, large areas of coral reef and atolls in the Indian and Pacific oceans have been bleached by increasingly warm water.

Additional threats to coral reefs come from other human activities, such as fishing – not just for food, but also for the international trade in tropical fish. The reefs themselves and the shells of snails and shellfish living among the reef are also plundered to satisfy the trade in souvenirs, jewellery and handicrafts and so collecting from coral reefs has been banned in some parts of the world.

In many countries, coral is mined from the reef and used to build houses and to make roads, or is burnt to make lime, and where this happens the consequences are often that reefs are stripped bare. The increase in tourist numbers can result in corals being trampled underfoot as the visitors walk out to the reef, destroying the very thing they have come to see; snorkellers and divers may kill polyps simply by touching coral colonies; and anchors and ship groundings can destroy large areas of reef.

Clear Cutting the Oceans

However, somewhat ironically it is the most recently discovered deep-sea corals that today are under the greatest threat from over fishing and deep sea oil drilling, both of which can cause untold damage to these fragile animals and their habitat.

It is not just the intensity of fishing which is a problem, but also the type of fishing. Some fishing techniques, such as bottom trawling and dredging, cause severe damage to seabed coral reefs and other habitats. Bottom trawling can reduce the sea floor to rubble in a matter of seconds. Deep-sea fishing, which is a relatively recent development, uses large nets, weighed down by steel balls that rip up everything in their path. This not only changes the sea floor into a desert, but it captures and destroys fish for which there is no commercial value. Heavy fishing around ocean seamounts or along the deep ocean shelf can completely destroy corals that have taken hundreds of years to grow. Recent observations on Ritchie seamount, a structure located off the east coast of New Zealand's North Island and heavily fished for a deep sea fish called the orange roughy, showed prominent 'gouges' caused by trawl doors.

Like the fishing industry, the oil and gas industry is moving into increasingly deeper oceans in the relentless search for more oil. Discharges of pollution from offshore drilling, as well as habitat destruction, pose direct threats to the fragile deep ocean ecosystem generally, and to deep-sea corals especially.

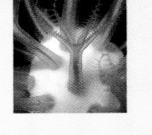

ABOVE The crown of thorns starfish, which can grow to 1m (40in) across devours coral polyps. Its only enemy is a large snail called triton. Collecting triton shells for souvenirs is one reason why the crown of thorns starfish populations have increased in some parts of the world with a subsequently devastating effect on the reef.

LEFT Global climate change is having a marked effect on the ocean world. Here coral reefs are bleached white as the water temperature is too high.

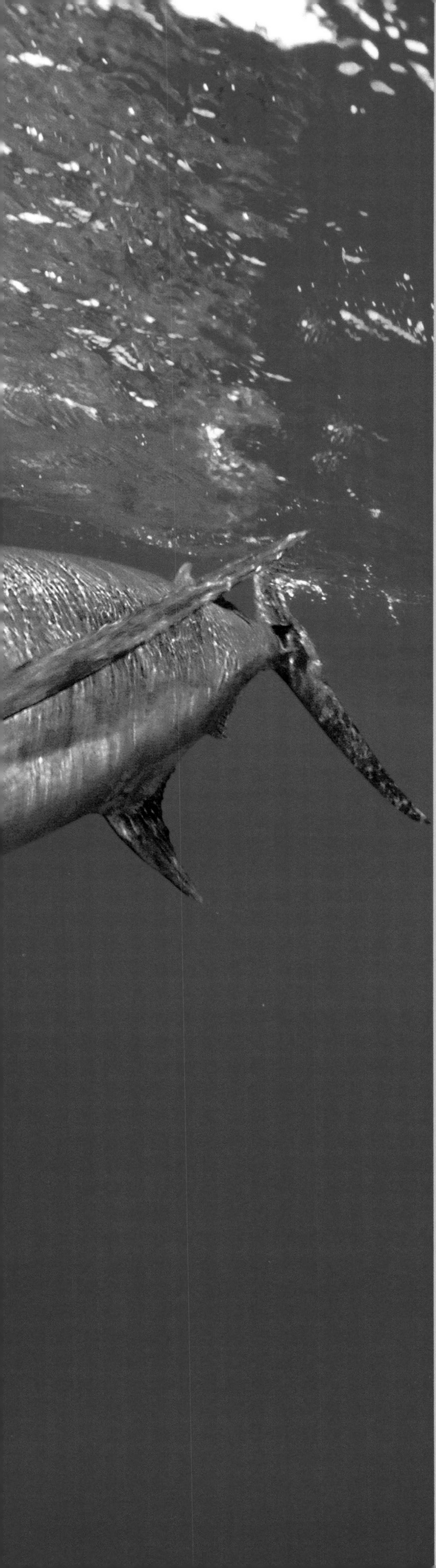

CHAPTER FOUR

FISH

The oceans teem with an infinite variety of fish of different sizes, shapes and colours, from the notorious sharks and rays, to flying fish, the flashing swordfish and marlin and countless other species. Fish have colonized practically every niche and habitat in the sea, from the seashore itself – where some can cope with being left out of water for short periods, including mud dwellers and rock crawlers – to the deepest oceans and the sea surface.

All fish have special senses, which they use to obtain information about their surroundings. On most fish there is a visible line of special scales running along each side of the body; this lateral line is in fact a small canal that runs just below the surface of the skin, and opens to the outside through tiny pores. The fluid in the canal moves with any movement in the water, which stimulates nerves to send a message to the brain. Others have a well developed sense of smell, and some fish can even generate their own electricity.

Every habitat in the sea has been colonised by fish. One of the largest fish, the marlin grows to 2½m (8ft) and has tremendous power and size. The upper jaw is pointed like a spear and they have a sharply forked tail.

Colour

The infinite variety of colours found in fish are used for camouflage, in sexual behaviour, and to enable them to recognize both their own species and those that live by cleaning parasites from the bodies of other fish.

Colour is possibly also used to recognize prey or predators. Clearly, therefore, fish have colour vision. To understand why and how colour works for different fish, we first need to know about how colour in the sea works: we need a fish's eye view.

Looking at the surface, the colour of the sea depends very much on the colour of the sky. For example, if the day is clear the sea will appear blue, whereas if it is a cloudy day the sea will look grey. Underwater, the colour depends very little on the weather: it is the colour of the water itself that is important. Pure water is blue, and places like the Mediterranean or the open ocean that don't contain a lot of suspended material, normally look blue. On the other hand, waters that surround more northern or southern coasts are green or yellow-green in colour.

Ordinary daylight is white, but it is composed of different colours or wavelengths, better known as the colours of the spectrum. When a narrow band of wavelengths is isolated or separated, such as happens in a rainbow, the eye sees the colours. The short wavelengths are the violet and blue end of the spectrum, longer wavelengths are the oranges and reds. Pure water absorbs all wavelengths of light, but the orange/red longer wavelengths are absorbed more quickly, and so it is the blue/green shorter wavelengths that penetrate deepest into a clear sea.

Coastal water in northern or southern regions appears green because of the amount of decaying vegetation that enters the sea from rivers, and the green chlorophyll present in plant plankton that is so abundant in certain seasons. The vegetation absorbs most light at the blue and violet end of the

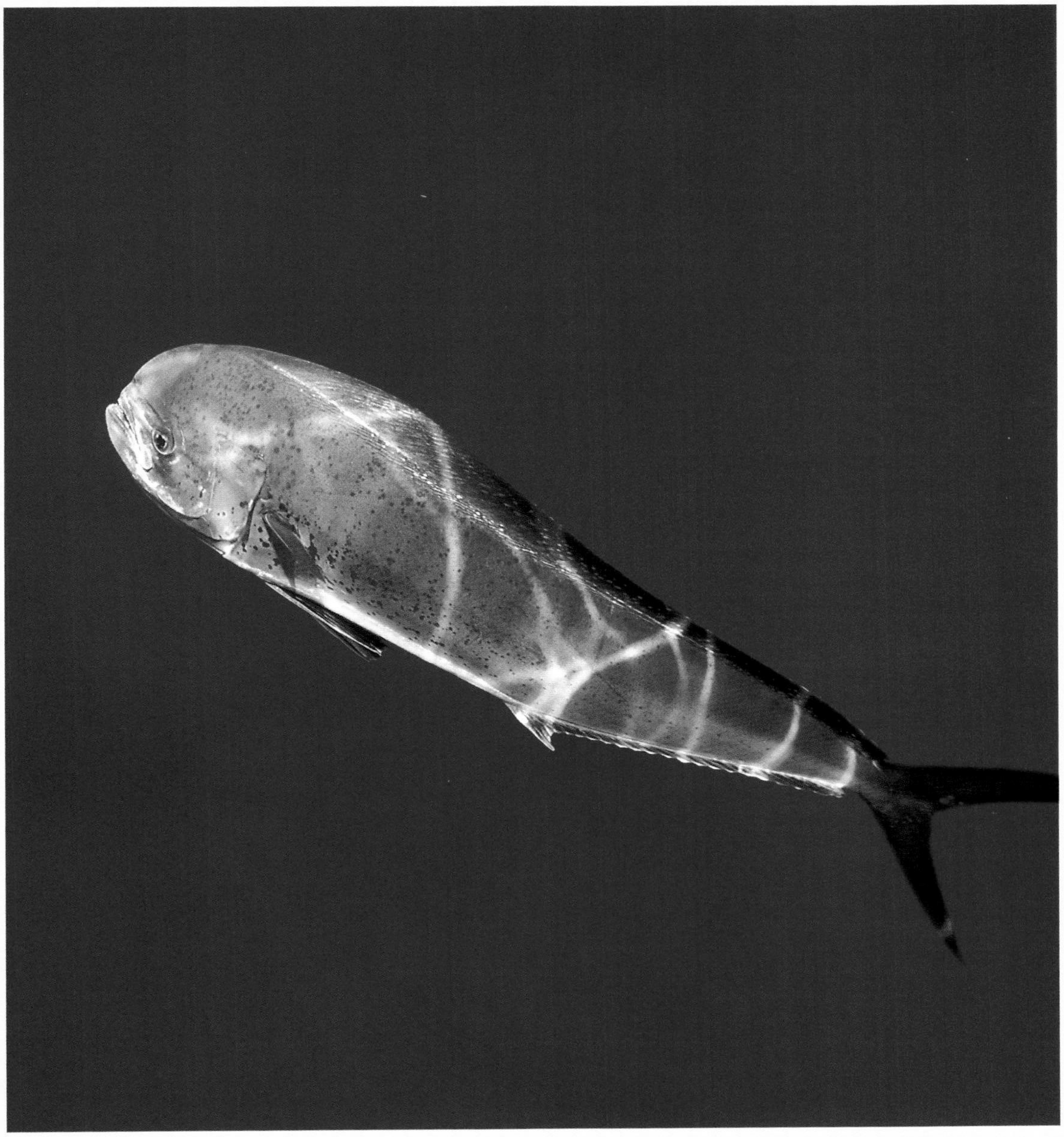

RIGHT The dorado, or dolphin fish, is characterized by spectacular colouring. This is achieved by pigment cells, and also by minute crystals in its scales that separate the light into a spectrum of different colours. These 2m (6½ft)-long fish are fast swimming, spectacular-looking fish, the body is blue-green above and silvery below, with silver and gold iridescence. Dorado feed on other fish and squid, and often leap out of the water in a frantic chase after flying fish. They usually live in shoals, and often undertake long breeding migrations.

OPPOSITE Because red light does not penetrate very deep, in clear water like the Mediterranean, red or pink fish (such as this gurnard) look grey or blue instead of the red they appear when brought to the surface.

spectrum, and the water itself absorbs the orange and red light, leaving the green and yellow light that penetrates deepest into the water.

Coloured objects do not look the same when viewed under water as they do on land, because the red light rays are almost non-existent at depths greater than about 20m (66ft), and in green water the violet and deep blue light is also absent. In practice, deep blue and yellow objects show up best in clear waters, and peacock blue and orange objects show up best in the green seas of the north and south.

Fish Colour

There are fishes of every known hue, from the brilliant reds and blues of the gurnards, to the muddy browns of many bottom-living flat fish. Some colours are conferred by tiny pigment-containing cells called chromatophores in the skin's surface that contain red, orange, yellow or black pigment. The pigmented area can expand and contract which, together with using different combinations of chromatophores, is responsible for most of the green, yellow, red, orange, brown and black colours of fishes.

Other colours, such as the silver, blue and iridescence of some fish, bass or marlin for example, are not produced by pigment, but by light passing through minute silvery crystals, called iridocytes, that are contained in the scales. Rather like light passing through a prism, the crystals separate the colours of the spectrum, and the precise arrangement of these crystals is essential for the correct colour. When the fish dies, the arrangement of crystals begins to break down, which is why the iridescent blue colouring of fishes is lost immediately after death, while the flanks of many open-water fish that are silver in life, present a rainbow of iridescent colours as they die. Most fish have both structural and pigmented colours, the pigment colours being responsible for the dark back, and the structural colours for the white and silvery flanks and belly.

Camouflage

The purpose of camouflage is, obviously, disguise. Imitating the surroundings can be done either by adopting the colours and even texture of the surroundings, by covering with sand, or just acting like a piece of rock.

Many fish in coastal waters imitate their surroundings. Pipefish swim vertically among eelgrass, their bodies swaying like the plants while other fish mimic overgrown rocks. Sargassum fish mimic their habitat by colour and by having fins which look like the weed among which they live (*see* chapter 8).

At sea, there is little to emulate except the water and sky and the silvery fish of open water can mimic both. Underwater, most light comes from above, but the amount of light in all horizontal directions is about equal so if a mirror is hung vertically in the sea it is almost invisible since the light reflected from it is the same as the light behind it. However, a fish is not flat but rounded and a simple mirrored surface would be useless as camouflage. The clever trick lies in tiny reflecting crystals in each fish scale that are so arranged over the body that the whole fish works like a vertical mirror.

Mirror camouflage does not work near the surface if there is a clear sky and a low sun when the light penetrates the water at an angle: under these conditions fishes swim with their backs slanted towards the sun. For perfect camouflage, silvery fishes must hold the correct position in the sea, for once their body tilts bright flashes of light are reflected from their flanks.

The system does not work when looking directly down or up at a fish and perfect camouflage against observation from below is not possible with this system as the fish appears as a dark silhouette. However, spotting a fish from above is made difficult by the chromatophores on the back that adjust the brightness and colour of the fish to match the light from below.

RIGHT TOP Silvery fish can mimic the sea and the sky. Mackerel hide by using counter-shading: from above, the dark and light blue stripes on its back match the water's ripples; its silver-white underside matches the brightly lit surface and, from the side, the body almost disappears as it reflects the colour of the water.

RIGHT The stonefish is very well camouflaged for both ambushing prey and protecting itself. They have an extremely venomous spine on the dorsal fin that can inflict a very painful and long-lasting wound that can be fatal.

Fish Types

There are essentially two groups of fish, separated according to their skeletons. Apart from these, there are primitive eel-like lampreys and hagfish, or snot-eels, that have a simple round mouth and horny teeth.

For the rest, those fish with a skeleton made from cartilage are in a class called chondrichthyes; these include the sharks, rays, sawfish, guitarfish and skates that are collectively known as 'elasmobranchs', meaning 'strap gills', referring to the five to seven gill slits found on each side of the head. The remaining fish have a skeleton made of bone and are classified as osteichthyes. Most of the world's bony fish are in a group called the teleost fish.

Sharks and Rays – Elasmobranchs

The sharks and rays are an ancient group of fishes. The earliest evidence of sharks comprises isolated spines, teeth and scales that appeared about 430 million years ago in the Silurian Period, known as the 'Age of Fishes.' For the last 100 million years they have remained almost unchanged and today there are about 400 different types of shark and 600

species of rays world-wide. About 100 shark species are commercially traded, but only about 12 are considered dangerous to humans. Sharks are among the world's most successful animals and are an important component of the natural marine environment, having evolved complex characteristics and behaviours. Many are migratory and different species occur in different habitats, including very deep oceans, the open sea, shallow coastal areas and, in some tropical regions; a few rarities even occur in lakes and rivers.

Some sharks and rays are tiny, able to fit on to the palm of your hand: the world's smallest shark is the Spined Pygmy or Dwarf Shark, *Squaliolus laticaudus*, which may reach 20cm (8in). Others are huge, such as the whale shark, *Rhincodon Typus* – this is the largest fish that ever existed that we know of, and can reach a length of almost 14m (46ft). The basking

RIGHT Lampreys and hagfish found in all temperate waters are primitive fish with a round mouth adapted to attaching to other fish and mammals from which they suck body fluids causing a round scar on the skin. Hagfish are slimy creatures living on the seafloor on any dead or dying animals and when caught they can fill a bucket with slime and water in a few seconds, hence their common name of snot-eels. Lampreys ascend rivers to spawn and the young spend their early lives feeding on rotting material in the river.

shark, *Cetorhinus maximus*, is the second largest fish in the sea, reaching lengths of about 10m (33ft).

Sharks have the same five senses that humans have, plus the ability to detect mild electric fields; this is valuable in finding prey, as both the environment and life forms create electric fields. In fact, sharks and rays were among the first animals to be discovered with the ability to detect electric fields, using their electro-receptive organs. These organs are usually clustered around the head, but they also may be spread out over the entire body surface. Different species have different arrangements of the electro-receptive organs; in fact, sometimes sharks may respond more rapidly to an electric field source than to the presence of smells or chemicals from a prospective food source in the water. Sharks have good vision with eyes similar to ours with a cornea, iris, pupil, lens and retina. Some even have a cover rather like an eye-lid that closes to protect the eye from any thrashing prey being eaten.

Unlike most bony fishes, sharks do not have well developed ribs or a swim bladder, which makes them slightly negatively buoyant. To compensate they have a large, oil-rich liver; but despite the lift provided by this, they will slowly sink unless they keep swimming. Their streamlined, cylindrical body shape reduces drag and requires a minimum of energy to swim; having a cartilage skeleton also helps because it is lighter than bone. It is also more flexible, which can only be an advantage when swimming and turning, and

ABOVE Sharks have good vision and nostrils that can detect the faintest smell. Teeth have different shapes depending on the food: the mako's teeth are pointed to grab and hold prey; the Great White's serrated triangular teeth cut chunks from the prey; the Nurse shark's conical teeth crush shellfish, crabs and lobsters. New teeth rotate forward to replace broken or worn teeth.

OPPOSITE The whale shark, *Rhincodon typus*, feeds by filtering small organisms from the water. The megamouth shark, another shark that feeds in the same way, is known only from less than ten specimens, and was first discovered in 1976.

many can turn virtually within their own length. However, the skeleton and fins are much less elaborately jointed than in bony fish, and this, combined with the lack of a swim bladder, means that the bodies of sharks are on the whole less manoeuvrable than those of many bony fish.

Plankton Eaters

Most sharks are flesh eaters, but the largest – the whale and basking sharks – feed like the baleen whales, filtering plankton and small fish from the water. The small prey are engulfed in the mouth, then filtered by the gills as the water passes out through the large gill slits. Whale sharks are lethargic animals, which might help to explain their occasional collisions with ships.

Smart Sharks

Contrary to popular belief, sharks are not stupid, and have well developed brains; indeed the brain weight to body weight ratios of some sharks exceed those for most bony fish, many birds, and even some mammals.

In deeper parts of the oceans, there are sharks of surprising forms and about which relatively little is known. One, dubbed the 'cookie cutter', has a round mouth with large wedge-shaped teeth on the bottom jaw that it uses to carve out plugs of meat from large fishes and marine mammals. The eyes in these deep-water sharks are often emerald green and adapted to perceive the luminescence of other animals that also dwell where sunlight never reaches. Other deep-dwelling sharks include the megamouth, goblin, frilled and pygmy sharks, which are hardly ever seen.

The Hunting Shark

In the natural world there are always fewer predatory animals than prey. The same is true in the oceans, and although sharks sometimes congregate in large numbers around boats or seamounts or near shoaling fish, when compared to the teeming millions of mackerel or herring, for example, they are a small percentage of the ocean's fish population.

Smell is probably the main hunting sense. A solitary shark cruising a shoreline will casually investigate anything floating by. The long twitching snout prospects for the scent of food, and any floating debris is given a nudge before a bite is taken if the sensory organs on the snout confirm the presence of food.

A quiescent shark will only snatch at prospective prey, which may or may not be successful, although the struggling of a live caught fish, for example, can increase the level of excitement: the shark will then make zigzag tracking movements, guided by its sense of smell, and will very quickly home in on the struggling fish. The hammerhead shark appears to have a particularly keen sense of smell, which is probably because the nostrils are very close to the eyes that are widely separated on the ends of the long projections on each side of the head. Thus this shark can locate the direction from which a scent comes with great accuracy.

If a feeding shark is approached by other sharks, a fierce competition can develop. Now any prospective food is not simply nudged, but taken into the mouth, and the other sharks will go for the same bait, resulting in a struggle. The commotion draws other sharks, which results in a feeding frenzy in which the sharks snap at each other, and any injured animals are instantly set upon.

Sharks and Humans

Despite their reputation, sharks seldom bite people. There are only about 50 to 75 known shark attacks world-wide a year, and very few of these are fatal; some half to three-quarters of recorded shark attacks have nothing to do with feeding activity.

Many more people are injured and killed each year by bee stings, snakes bites, crocodiles or tigers than by sharks. Furthermore, most shark attacks appear to result from mistaken identity, such as when a swimmer is among fish on which a shark is feeding, when the shark believes it is repelling an intruder, or when a person bumps into, steps on, or otherwise disturbs a shark.

Large open water sharks such as the oceanic white-tip, the mako, the blue, and the white shark, all of which sometimes feed on large prey, have been implicated in fatal shark attacks. For swimmers in the Gulf of Mexico, potentially the most dangerous sharks are the tiger shark, the hammerheads, the lemon shark and the aggressive bull shark that will enter brackish water and sometimes even fresh water. Despite this potential, there are still relatively few incidents. So while it is true that a few sharks eat people, many more people eat sharks and their harvesting is a clear threat to their long history of survival that, in turn, puts at risk the shark's unique role in the marine ecosystem.

Life History

Sharks tend to live a long time, sometimes up to 70 years; they also grow slowly, and do not mature until they are 20 – 25 years old in some species, and almost 30 years in the case of the sandbar shark. Sharks and rays have developed reproductive strategies that are very similar to those of other large mammals that have few natural predators. Partly because being top predators, and therefore relatively fewer in number, they have evolved breeding patterns especially geared to ensure that their offspring have the best chance of survival.

In contrast to the mass spawnings of most fish, where huge numbers of eggs are shed into the sea, the larger sharks have relatively few (from four to ten, depending on the species), large young, produced after a pregnancy of a year or more.

Some are migratory, following warm waters to higher latitudes in summer, and then retreating again at the beginning of winter, and most of these species probably have breeding grounds where males and females congregate to mate. For the large open-ocean species, such as the great white, mako and blue sharks, such an arrangement is needed otherwise many would never find a mate. All sharks go to great lengths to protect their developing young before birth.

ABOVE Sharks' large front pectoral fins provide lift. Usually the top lobe of the tail fin is longer, but in the fast predatory sharks, like this great white, the tail fins are symmetrical.

LEFT A rare photograph of nurse sharks mating in the Atlantic Ocean off the Florida Keys.

OPPOSITE TOP Approximately 40% of sharks lay eggs; the others give birth. In the egg the embryo, attached to its yolk, is in a horny case. The young hatches when the yolk is used up.

OPPOSITE Pregnant sharks select nurseries that will provide the best conditions for their young. Some nurseries are well known, for example new born bull sharks grow up in the shallow bays and estuaries of the northern Gulf of Mexico

ABOVE Shallow waters are visited by open ocean species of shark, and are home to bottom feeders such as the wobbegong, found in the Western Pacific around Indonesia, Papua New Guinea, and northern Australia.

Although mating sharks have rarely been observed, it is known that they reproduce by internal fertilisation. In the case of dogfish, which have been seen mating, the slender male fish wraps itself around the female. This is not practicable for the large sharks where the males have claspers, some also with a formidable array of hooks and gaffs to secure the female. It would seem, from the scars on the females resulting from mating, that considerable coercion is needed. However, despite the male's apparently vicious behaviour, the mating season is probably more hazardous to them than females. While on the breeding grounds, it appears that males do not feed and can become extremely thin with the oil content of their livers falling to almost nothing. Since males are usually about 25 per cent smaller than the females, and perhaps their typical aggressiveness is inhibited by the need to mate, a male can be killed by an unwilling female.

Sharks have no scales – their skin is made up of small pointed structures, called dermal denticles, that point backwards to reduce friction, and which give the characteristic feel of shark-skin. Sharks inhabit all seas and some freshwater lakes, with bays or estuaries serving as nursery grounds for many juveniles. Shark migration may be long or short, and is determined by food availability or reproductive cycles. The bull shark, *Carcharhinus leucas*, cruises along the continental shelves but is uniquely adapted to freshwater, inhabiting Lake Nicaragua. It has been found in rivers 3,200km (2,000 miles) inland.

Skates, Rays and their Kin – Batoids

Skates and rays are flattened from top to bottom – an adaptation to living on the seafloor. Flatfish, such as plaice and flounders, are also flat, but from side-to-side, which develops in the young when one eye migrates over the head; the side with both eyes becomes the pigmented 'upper' side, while the other becomes the 'lower' side. Some rays, like the stingrays, have defensive, venomous spines on the tail, which can inflict a very painful, though rarely fatal, wound. Skates swim, using undulations of the edges of the fins, just above the seabed, keeping their height to a minimum to avoid being spotted by predators. Their flat body, together with their camouflaged back, makes them difficult to see when lying on, or partially buried in, the seabed.

Both skates and rays can extend their jaws like forceps to grasp prey from the seafloor. Skates have pointed teeth and feed on shrimps, worms and flatfish. Stingrays have flat, cobblestone-like teeth for crushing crabs, whereas eagle rays have hard molar-like plates that can crush the shells of molluscs such as oysters and snails.

Some rays do not live on the seabed but feed in the ocean. These oceanic rays, such as the Eagle, Cownose and Manta Rays, evolved relatively recently, dating from the lower Eocene period, about 55 million years ago, whereas their seabed-dwelling cousins can be dated to the lower Jurassic period, about 200 million years ago. The pectoral fins of oceanic rays are like wings, and they 'fly' through the water and use their front horn-like fins to funnel water laden with plankton into the mouth. Mantas often leap out of the water and somersault before landing with a loud smack or they just bask lazily on the surface. They have eyes on the sides of the head, very small teeth and a small fin towards the rear.

Skates have cusped teeth, one or two dorsal fins and sharp spines along their backs whereas rays have flat plate-like teeth and the dorsal fin is either absent, near the rear or in some species it forms a long fin-fold. The key difference is that rays give birth while skates lay eggs in a rectangular leathery case, like some of the smaller sharks and dogfish. The egg case has long threads to anchor it among the shallow water seaweed. When empty and washed up on the shore it is known as a mermaid's purse.

Ray embryos stay inside their mother throughout their development. They finish their yolk about halfway through the pregnancy and are then fed with a protein-rich bath called uterine milk. In some eagle rays, the 'milk' is pumped directly into the cavity behind the mouth of each developing ray. Perhaps most intriguingly of all, some rays, notably the eagle and manta rays, have proportionately the largest brains of any elasmobranch, and show complex social behaviour.

Bony Fish – Teleosts

Most fish are bony fish. Unlike sharks and rays they have a bone skeleton, a cover over their gills and most have scales, though some have lost them during evolution. Fish are found everywhere in the oceans and some, like salmon and eels, live in both sea and in freshwater rivers and lakes. Others have adapted to cope with the daily changes in the salinity of river estuaries and deltas. Deep-sea fish tend to be dark or red; their velvety scales reflect no light, so they are practically invisible in their natural habitat.

ABOVE The manta rays and devil fish found in the tropical and sub-tropical oceans, are frighteningly large, with a wing span of 6m (20ft), yet harmless. Eagle rays, seen here, are smaller, but just as spectacular.

BELOW Electric rays have simple grasping teeth, but they can stun prey or discourage predators, using modified gill muscles that can generate up to 220 volts of electricity. Fishermen may receive a shock from a line after hooking an electric ray.

Contact and Communication

On land, animals find food, enemies and mates mainly by using eyes, ears and smell. In the sea, senses are also needed, and fish are neither silent nor deaf, as they both hear and generate sounds that travel very efficiently through water.

In some ways a fish's inner ear is similar to ours, and is situated near the front at the end of the lateral line. Although limited in the ways they can produce sound, they can still produce a range of noises: for instance swimming and feeding sounds, such as parrotfish or triggerfish crunching on coral. Others are able to rub their teeth or fins together, or can force water out of their gills; a method only available to fish with air bladders is to use specialized muscles to beat the swim bladder like a drum.

While it has long been known that fish communicate by means of grunts, squeaks and whistles in order to mark their territory and find a mate, recent studies have shown that some fish call to their young: the young fish are sent by their parent fish away from the reef into the open sea as a way to avoid predators. When they are big enough to return, their parents call them back into the reef. Perhaps one of the most unusual sounds is emitted by herring. They produce a high-pitched

sound by squeezing air out of the anus – in other words, they communicate by farting.

The density of water makes it a better medium than air for transmitting small rhythmic pressure changes caused by vibrations. Hence fish have an added sense: the lateral line, which enables them to detect and respond to vibrations caused by moving objects in the water.

An Eye for Detail

However sensitive the nose is, most fish depend on their eyes for spotting and capturing their food. Their eyes have a structure similar to those in land animals, although modified because of the different medium in which they are used. For instance, they have no need for eyelids or tear glands to keep the surface of the eye moist and clean. Many have eyes on each side of the head that can move independently of each other, giving a wide field of vision all round. The front of the eye, the cornea, is nearly flat, but behind it is a large spherical lens that focuses light on to the sensitive retinal layer that lines the eyeball. Hence both the position and the shape of the eyes enable a fish to see clearly objects close in front of it, which is useful for sighting nearby food, friends or enemies. To the sides, it can see further, and is aware of fairly distant movements.

Fish living on the seabed at great depths have limited vision, but they have compensatory alternative senses. Like the majority of fish, they have scales, but these tend to be thin and the skin contains many sense organs that give the body an all-over sensitivity to contact. The tripod fish 'walks' about on the bottom on three long projections from the pelvic fins and tail that contain sense organs to detect food in the mud.

The fish with the largest eyes are those species that spend most of their lives in the mid-water zone at depths of between 100 and 1,000m (300 – 3,000ft). Only a small amount of light penetrates this twilight region where most objects appear green or blue in clear water. Mid-water animals have large pupils and lenses which can focus the small amount of light into a pinpoint to give the clearest picture possible. The retina of such fish is particularly sensitive to blue and green light and there is often an extra reflecting layer, which causes the fish's eyes to shine like those of a cat caught in the headlights of a car.

Animals that normally live below 1,000m (3,000ft), whether swimming freely or lying on the bottom, exist in almost total darkness and have small eyes. The fact that they have eyes at all suggests that they are aware of

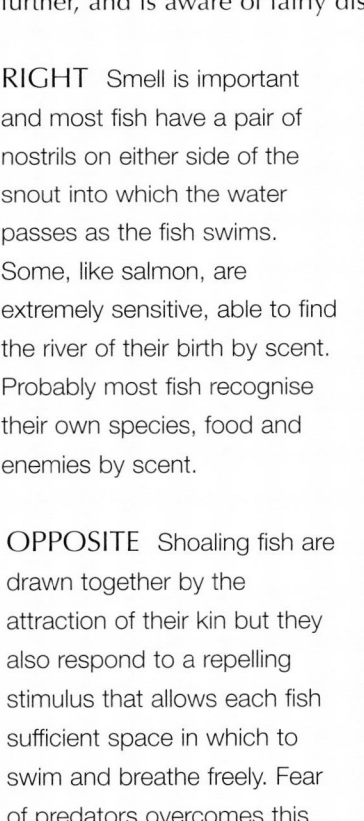

RIGHT Smell is important and most fish have a pair of nostrils on either side of the snout into which the water passes as the fish swims. Some, like salmon, are extremely sensitive, able to find the river of their birth by scent. Probably most fish recognise their own species, food and enemies by scent.

OPPOSITE Shoaling fish are drawn together by the attraction of their kin but they also respond to a repelling stimulus that allows each fish sufficient space in which to swim and breathe freely. Fear of predators overcomes this second stimulus and allows them to pack together more tightly. There is remarkable communication in a shoal, with each fish changing direction simultaneously.

luminous objects around them, but the poorly developed eyes are only simple receptors sensitive to changes in light intensity, but deficient in detailed vision. This is because a fish living on the seabed, at whatever depth, is more likely than a free-swimming fish to find organisms on which to feed without searching for them. Thus creatures such as the rattails and eelpouts have absolutely no need for big eyes, because they spend their entire lives within 1 –2m (3 – 6ft) of the seabed.

Dangerous Friends, Mutual Help

In the sea survival can depend on different animals cooperating and relationships may be mutually rewarding, or it may be that only one benefits. For example, pilot fish, *Naucrates ductor*, swim with sharks, turtles, and rays clearly getting protection from their host. On the other hand the relationship between the Portuguese Man-of-War and the fish, *Nomeus*, could be mutually beneficial as the fish, which lives unharmed beneath the Man-of-War and is even camouflaged to blend in with the

LEFT This shrimp may look to be dicing with death in getting so close to the moray eel's mouth, but it is a cleaner shrimp that picks off dead skin and parasites from the eel so the animals benefit each other.

BELOW Often seen swimming close to sharks is a small fish called the pilot fish. *Naucrates ductor*, which only grows to 35 – 70cm (13 – 27in) long. This fish is also associated with turtles, mantas, boats and even drifting debris. Initially, it was thought that they ate parasites from their large hosts or even helped themselves to titbits after the host had eaten. But it is more likely that the fish are simply getting shelter and protection from larger predators. Young pilot fish can often be found hiding beneath larger jellyfish.

BELOW Shark suckers or remoras have a ridged disc on top of the head that looks like the sole of a boot and is a fin modified as a sucker. It attaches to sharks, manta rays, turtles, large fish and even boats. Remoras do not suck body fluids from their host, but mostly feed on parasites. Young remoras first attach themselves while only 3 or 4cm (1 – 1½in) long, often to an adult remora, but they change hosts as they grow. Some are very particular about which host they choose; *Remora brachyptera* attaches to swordfish or marlins, while *Remora albescens* prefers manta rays.

tentacles, gets protection from larger predators and it may attract fish on which the Man-of-War then feeds.

Some fish put on displays when they need attention, such as the mullet or goatfish, which indicate that they need cleaning by standing on their heads. Their cleaner fish, a small striped wrasse, then carefully goes over the larger fish, removing parasites and infected tissues from the scales, fins and mouth. The wrasse advertises itself by bright colours and often has a regular corner of the reef as a cleaning station.

Hide, Fight, Frighten or Flight

The continuous competition between predator and prey has led to the evolution of many kinds of defence. Like land animals, marine creatures defend themselves by hiding, fighting, frightening or by taking flight.

Some fish choose hiding as a form of defence. The blenny, for example, hides in caves and empty shells, and eels bury themselves in the sand. Some fish rely on camouflage, while yet others simply rely on being difficult to see – for instance, cardinal fish have various patterns of conspicuous black and white stripes and spots that break up their body outline and make them difficult to recognize as fish. Most animals with zebra stripes, like the sergeant-major fish, exemplify this disruptive effect. Such vivid patterns are normally found among tropical fish living in shallow, clear water where visibility is good. The huge numbers of different types of fish found on coral reefs (*see* Chapter 3), has led to the development of some of the most spectacular colours, shapes

and patterns, and methods of camouflage employed in order to avoid being eaten. It has also been observed that, as opposed to blending into the background, having conspicuous colouring is an effective defence.

Safety in Numbers

For fish with no built-in weapons against predators, a communal life provides the best protection. When living together in a large shoal, hidden in the crowd, an individual has a much better chance of avoiding an enemy than if it were alone. Herring, mackerel, anchovies and other shoaling fish swim together in their thousands. Another advantage to the concentration of many fish into one small area is that there is

LEFT The dragon or lion fish has long wing-like fins and gaudy stripes. Its fantastic shape is a warning, discouraging other animals from coming close. If a predator is not put off by its appearance and seizes the fish, it receives a painful or even fatal wound from venom injected by the spines on the fish's back.

OPPOSITE This porcupine puffer fish has a body like an inflatable pin-cushion that protects it from all but the most aggressive attackers. Other fish weapons include armoured plates like the trunk fish, and the surgeon fish has its own flick-knife in its tail that can spring out when needed.

rear pelvic fins, are elongated so they resemble and operate harm's way. Their front (pectoral) fins and, in some species, the using a sculling action of the lower lobe of the tail, glide out of by launching out of the sea and, after taxiing across the surface temperate oceans of the world, and they can escape predators Flying fish are found in all tropical, sub-tropical and warm

Flying Fish

Some fish can literally take flight from chasing predators.

defence of territories and/or mates.
body structure and behaviour, including aggressive and violent live. This has resulted in a wide range of mechanisms in both themselves and different species, for both food and a place to hand, have to cope with a lot of competition between is escape from predators. Small fish on coral reefs, on the other the living space is the open ocean, where a key factor There are about 4,000 different species of shoaling fish, and detect shoals of fish over a mile away using their echolocation. birds over a wide area see and join it. As for whales, they can when one gull or gannet plunges to a shoal it has found, other dealing with this problem. Birds have excellent eyesight and hunters such as whales and seabirds have their own ways of less chance of them being found in the ocean. However,

have no difficulty in sensing when and in which direction to turn. neighbours because of the lateral line sense organ. Even blind fish fish, like these sardines, is aware of any changes in direction of its maintain their position and stay evenly spaced in the shoal. Each

ABOVE Shoaling fish use their eyes and the lateral line organ to

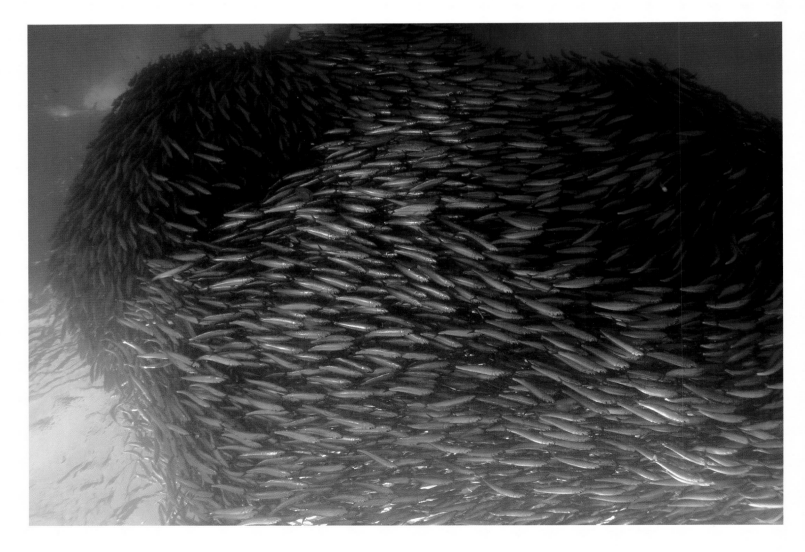

Out of the Blue

like wings. Generally the oceanic species are two-winged and grow to about 20cm (8in), while the better fliers are the larger and more coastal four-winged species that may grow to 40cm (16in). Both species swim just below the surface with their wings folded along the body.

Four-wingers may cover up to 300m (980ft) over the water, although normal flights usually cover 30 – 100m (100 – 330ft). Usually they glide about one or two metres above the surface, but they have been reported hitting a ship's bridge-wing 11m (36ft) above the sea. They are attracted to light, and this characteristic is used to catch them in some parts of the world. It also partly explains their frequent appearance on the decks of ships in the morning, where they can be collected to make an excellent breakfast.

A Need for Speed

Out in the ocean there are many fast-swimming fish, including scads, yellow-tails and jacks. These voracious hunters are seldom found below 100m (330ft) depth, and are widely distributed in tropical and temperate waters. Many, especially the young and smaller species, have the habit of sheltering around large floating objects. Fast swimmers include the dolphin fish, marlins, spearfish and sailfish that are found in tropical and sub-tropical waters and can grow in excess of two metres (6ft). These fish feed on other fish and squid, and often leap out of the water in a frantic chase after flying fish.

Swordfish can reach a length of 3.5m (11½ft), and are similar to marlins, although the upper jaw is flat, not cylindrical, and the fin does not extend down the body.

Neither marlin nor swordfish use their long jaws to spear food, but rather lash out among shoals of fish and then return to eat the dead and injured ones. The fastest fish in the sea, which is also the largest tuna, is the bluefin tuna, *Thunnus thynnus*, with a recorded speed of over 70km/h (44.5mph) over a 20 second dash, and reported bursts of speed of over 100km/h (60mph). Its body has slots into which it can fold down its dorsal and pectoral fins. The 'drive train' of the tuna is a crescent-shaped tail that is moved from side to side by powerful muscles. Unlike most fish, which use the majority of the after-part of their bodies in swimming, the tuna propels itself only with its tail.

Not only is this fish the fastest swimmer, it also makes one of the longest migrations of any fish: specimens tagged in the Bahamas have been recaptured in Newfoundland, Norway, and even Uruguay. The northern bluefin ranges across the North Pacific, migrating from California to Japan and back, sometimes detouring as far south as Papua New Guinea. The southern bluefin, *Thunnus maccoyii*, makes similar parallel migrations in the southern hemisphere. Along the way, bluefins feed on mackerel, herring, mullet, whiting, eels and squid.

Unfortunately for the bluefin, its dark red, muscular flesh is regarded as one of the most desirable of all fish products, and it can fetch a high price. This has led to tremendous fishing pressure that has seriously reduced its numbers, and the rarer the bluefin, the higher the price: fishing pressure is therefore relentless. It is but one of many victims of pure market economics. The fishing pressure on other tuna, including albacore, yellowfin, bigeye and skipjack, has also brought these fish on to the endangered list.

The slow growth and long lifespan of this species – it does not reach maturity until at least eight years of age, and has a lifespan of about 40 years – make it extremely vulnerable to overfishing, and slow to recover from stock reductions.

Perhaps the complete antithesis to the mighty tuna is the strange but nevertheless impressive sunfish, *Mola mola*, found in the open oceans of tropical and temperate areas. At 3m (10ft) across they are one of the largest of the bony fish, but very little is known about them. They are not common, although they have been hunted with harpoons in the past in places like the Aran Islands off the west coast of Ireland, which would seem to indicate that they were more numerous in the past.

Sunfish are shaped like a large disc with a leathery skin, no scales and the tail-fin is a frill running down the blunt rear end. Both the dorsal and anal fins are narrow and greatly elongated. Despite its size, it has a small mouth with large fused teeth rather like a single beak-like tooth in each jaw. They are probably deep-sea fish as when they are seen at the surface they are swimming feebly on their sides.

69

OPPOSITE Tuna are among the fastest fish in the sea, with the record being held by the mighty blue-fin. The fish undertake some of the longest migrations of all fish, wandering across the North and South Pacific and the Atlantic Ocean into the Mediterranean Sea. Tuna, sometime referred to as 'chicken of the sea', outsells all other types of canned fish or meat, with 3.3 billion cans sold worldwide and is under further attack from illegal 'pirate' fishing fleets seeking to capitalise on the spiralling price of tuna in Japan.

ABOVE Sunfish, *Mola mola*, which can grow to 3m (10ft) in diameter, are found in the open oceans of tropical and temperate areas. These sedate, mysterious fish normally live at depths of 180 – 360m (600 – 1,200ft) and eat small jellyfish, sea squirts and sea gooseberries. Very little is known about their life cycles, how they reproduce or how long they live and, although they are not commonly seen today, they may have been more abundant in the past.

Courtship and Breeding

In sea, as on land, a male must usually first establish his territory by showing himself in it and driving away intruders. He must then attract a female, and stimulate her to mate.

Establishing a territory in the open ocean can be somewhat fraught. Some male fish use their colours to establish a territory and signal their readiness to mate, and in shallow well-lit water or within a close-knit shoal, finding a mate is not difficult. However in the darkness of the deep-sea, finding a partner is difficult. Many of these fish have evolved distinctive patterns of luminous organs on their bodies making it easier to identify members of the opposite sex. For example, male and female lantern fish (*see* page 103) have different patterns of luminescent organs on their bodies.

Together Forever

One way to ensure regular mating in the deep ocean is to establish a permanent relationship once you have found your partner. When a young male angler, less than one-third the size of the female, finds a female, he sinks his teeth into her head and hangs on. The skin of his jaws joins to the female, most of his organs degenerate and the two bloodstreams become continuous and so he becomes a parasite, totally dependent on his mate – he gets food and a place to live, she is guaranteed fertilisation of her eggs.

Another solution to the predicament of finding and keeping a mate is simply to be both sexes in one, that is to become a hermaphrodite. This is very rare in fish, but it does exist in the small deep sea fish, *Benthalbella*.

What of the Offspring?

Breeding consumes a lot of energy and growing up in the oceans is hazardous as both the sea and predators take an enormous toll. If you are not around to take care of the young, the energy is used to produce large numbers of eggs and sperm, thereby ensuring that at least some offspring will grow to maturity. Herring lay tens of thousands of eggs a year whereas some angler fish lay approximately a million; the eggs and young fish are an important part of the plankton. Alternatively the energy can be spent in migrating to nursery areas and selecting safe places to lay eggs. A third strategy is to stay and protect your offspring, in which case it is not necessary to produce a huge number of eggs. Many sharks and rays adopt the latter strategy.

OPPOSITE TOP Flamboyance marks the courtship behaviour of the male dragonet, a bottom-living fish in shallow coastal waters, who fans out his brilliant fins before the nearest female. When she responds by moving towards him, he supports her on his broadly spread pelvic fins as they swim together up to the surface where the eggs are laid and fertilized.

OPPOSITE BOTTOM In the breeding season, the cuckoo wrasse of the north Atlantic, whose normal colour is a subdued pattern of blues and greens, takes on a rainbow effect with dramatic increase in colours. He shows off his new colours in a spectacular courtship display to the plain, pinkish-brown female.

LEFT In seahorses and the closely related pipefish, it is the male who looks after the young. The female deposits her eggs in a brood pouch on the underside of the male's body. After fertilization the eggs are retained in the pouch, nourished by special substances produced by the male. After a few weeks the fully formed young emerge and cling to surrounding weeds, looking just like miniature versions of their parents.

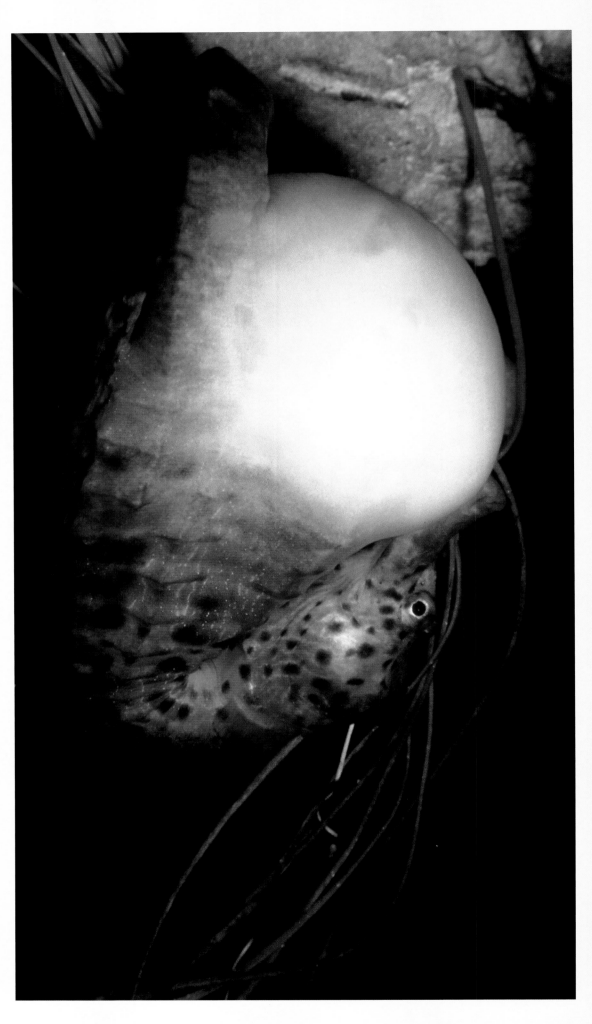

Out of the Blue

CHAPTER FIVE

WHALES, DOLPHINS, PORPOISES AND SEALS

They say the sea is cold;
but the sea contains the hottest blood of all.

D.H. Lawrence

The marine mammals, and these include dolphins and porpoises, range from the smallest seal, which grows to less than a metre (3ft), to the largest animal ever to have lived – the blue whale, which may reach 30m (100ft) in length. Mammals, like us, are warm blooded, in that their body maintains the same temperature regardless of any changes outside, and they give birth to young that are fed with milk produced by the mammary glands. The whales, dolphins and seals represent our closest relatives in the sea.

Marine mammals – whales, dolphins, porpoises and seals – have successfully colonised all oceans and seas from the poles to the tropics.

Cetaceans: Whales, Dolphins and Porpoises

This group of marine mammals has lost all connection with the land. They eat, mate and give birth entirely in the sea. Seals, on the other hand, must return to the land, or ice, to breed.

Life, it is believed, originated in the sea some 3,000 million years ago, but it wasn't until about 350 million years ago that some animals moved on to the land. From these primitive life forms all living things evolved. Mammals developed on land, but the ancestors of today's marine mammals probably lived in muddy regions near the sea, from which they got their food; over time they evolved until they had a full marine lifestyle having gradually lost their back limbs and developed a horizontal tail flipper or fluke. The front limbs were retained and developed into the flippers. The animals are streamlined and all projections such as nipples and external ears are enclosed in a fold of skin or have been lost altogether. Even the penis, which may be up to 3m (6ft) long in the large whales, is

held back in a fold of the skin by muscles attached to what remains of the back limbs. Evolution has made these mammals into very efficient swimmers with perhaps the only drawback being that they still need to surface to breathe air. In whales and dolphins the 'nose' has developed far back on the head, so it is the first thing to break the surface. They have also developed the ability to breathe out and in very quickly; for example, the fin whale exchanges over 3,000 times the air volume of a human in less than two seconds.

Whales and their relatives are divided into two distinct groups, depending on whether they have teeth – the Odontocetes – or whalebone (also called baleen) – the Mysticetes. The number of teeth that the Odontocetes have

OPPOSITE Baleen or whalebone whales like this humpback are the largest whales. The baleen or whalebone looks like a system of brushes hanging from the roof of the mouth and acts like a giant sieve to filter food from the water. The whale takes in a huge mouthful of water laden with plankton, then squeezes the water out through the baleen, trapping the food on the inside.

ABOVE A whale's 'blow' is a cloud of vapour mainly produced by condensation when warm breath comes into contact with cooler air. It is, therefore distinct in the colder Polar Regions, but it is equally dramatic in warmer areas because the air is expelled very quickly and when a gas that has been under pressure expands, it cools and the water condenses, even in the tropics.

ranges from one, in beaked whales, to 200 in some dolphins. There are about 80 different species of whales, dolphins and porpoises, 10 of which are the baleen or whalebone whales, the remainder are toothed whales, most of which are dolphins and porpoises. The exact number of species is a continuing source of debate, as they are distributed all over the world. For example, there are northern and southern varieties that have evolved slight differences, and some scientists identify these as separate species while others prefer to call them 'sub-species' or 'varieties'. Some, such as the beaked whales, are very rare, and one, the IndoPacific or Longman's beaked whale, *Indopacetus pacificus*, was only known from two skull samples, one found in 1882 and the other in 1968, and from other fragmentary remains found in South Africa, the Maldives and Kenya. However, in December 2002, a dead one was found beached in Japan, which provided some more information about this animal.

'Thar She Blows!'

This is the famous cry from the lookout when a whale is spotted. The whales give themselves away through their very obvious and distinctive 'blow'. This has a different shape for each species, and experienced whalers can identify whales purely from the shape of the blow. A blue whale produces a tall fountain of mist when it surfaces; a right whale produces a double blow that forms a V shape; while sperm whales have a blow that points forward and at an angle to one side.

The California grey whales, with their regular pattern of migration and the proximity of their habitat to the west coast of North America, were vulnerable to hunters. In the mid-nineteenth century the population was estimated at about 30,000, but the whaling industry reduced numbers so much that it became unprofitable by the end of the century. A resumption of whaling in the 1920s and 1930s brought the animals to the point of extinction, but eventually, in 1937, they were protected by law. Since then, the numbers of the California grey have increased, stabilizing at about 11,000. The Asia grey whale has not fared so well, however, and numbers are now extremely low.

Like other whales, the greys and humpback whales are very active and regularly leap out of the water and crash back, activity known as breaching; this behaviour probably serves to remove irritating barnacles and whale lice. Occasionally greys will stand with just their heads poking out of the sea, apparently looking around. This spy-hopping is also characteristic of the Orcas.

The right whales, which include the bowheads, were the basis of the large industrial whaling industry. The Greenland right whale, or bowhead, was described as the common

ABOVE The most primitive baleen whales are the greys. California greys migrate along the North American coast from Alaska, to Mexico whereas the Asian grey migrates from the sea of Japan to the Okhotsk Sea off the Russian Far East. It is today's most endangered species.

whale, but it is now one of the rarest. These whales, and their almost identical relative, the southern right whale, may grow to 16m (52ft). They have horny outgrowths called callosities on the front of the jaws. The northern right whale in the Atlantic is found from the Denmark Strait to the Caribbean and from the Norwegian Sea to the Canary Isles, and in the Pacific from the Sea of Japan, to the northern ocean and down the west coast of the US. The southern right whale is found throughout the southern ocean with concentrations around western Australia, New Zealand, Chatham Island, southern Chile and southwest Africa.

Breathing

Most of the baleen whales feed at or near the surface, and do not usually dive very deep or for very long; three or four breaths are usually enough to replenish their oxygen before the next dive, which is usually between five and ten minutes. Sperm whales seldom dive for less than 30 minutes, and so spend longer on the surface replenishing their oxygen supplies. They breathe about once for every minute spent on a dive.

ABOVE The sperm whale's head incorporates the spermaceti organ, which contains a fine oil that is solid when cool, through which runs the nasal passage up to 5m (15ft) long. Water in the nasal passage may cool and solidify the oil, making the head heavier and neutrally buoyant in cold deep water. On the surface warm blood makes the oil less waxy and the head lighter. This may be conjecture but the curious head structure is certainly remarkable.

RIGHT Whales have very efficient lungs and breathing ability. They carry much of the oxygen in the muscles as well as the blood and they can withstand pressures by collapsing their lungs so they can re-surface rapidly without suffering the human dive problem of the 'bends'.

For animals that breathe air, the diving ability of whales is truly remarkable. Even though some can stay under water for more than an hour at a time, their lungs are not particularly large. Relative to body size, our lungs are larger than a whale's, making up about seven per cent of our bodyweight, whereas in the large whales the lungs are only about three per cent of their bodyweight. But whales make much more efficient use of their lungs than we do: we breathe in only about half a litre (one pint) of air, despite the fact that our lungs have a volume of more than four litres (seven pints). Whales, on the other hand, fill their lungs to capacity each breath, and they change up to 90 per cent of the air supply each time.

But the efficient use of their lungs does not fully account for the fact that they can hold their breath for up to 20 times longer than any terrestrial animal. Air-breathing animals take oxygen into the lungs, which is then transferred to the bloodstream and round the body to the muscles and tissues that need it. Thus most of the oxygen in our bodies is dissolved in the blood – but a whale about to dive has up to 40 per cent of its oxygen supply locked up in its muscles. The massive amount of oxygen bound in the muscles gives whale meat a characteristic dark colour that can be almost black.

Deep-diving whales also need to cope with great pressures. Sperm and bottlenose whales are the deepest divers, and they must be able to withstand pressures often as great as 300 atmospheres (300 times that at the surface), which would crush most terrestrial animals. They can return rapidly from such great pressures without suffering from any of the compressed-air problems such as getting the 'bends', which can kill human divers. The bends are caused if a diver surfaces too quickly, and nitrogen, a major component of air, that had dissolved in the blood under increased water pressure, is suddenly released, forming bubbles in the bloodstream and causing pain – the 'bends' – and paralysis.

Obviously whales do not breathe compressed air, but before diving the whale takes 30 or 40 breaths – that is, they hyperventilate, which is something a human diver must never do – and go down with one lungful that does not contain enough nitrogen to produce the 'bends'. They avoid the risk of absorbing even this small amount by simply allowing their chest to cave in, so that below 100m (330ft) the lungs are collapsed, and all the air they contain has been forced into the windpipe and nasal passages where no nitrogen can be absorbed.

But there is nothing left over for emergencies. We exchange about 15 per cent of lung capacity when breathing normally; under stress we can take a deep breath and pick up enough extra oxygen for a special effort. Whales cannot do this – their lungs are already at capacity, so they can only get more air by breathing on the surface. They can pant, but not with their

ABOVE Orcas feed on fish, seals, and other cetaceans and will even chase seals onto beaches and risk getting stranded. They will take calves of large whales and even bites out of the adults. Orcas off the west coast of the US often ambush grey whales, working together to separate calves from their mothers.

OPPOSITE Humpbacks, which can reach 16m (52ft), catch fish in bubble nets. The whale dives and surrounds a fish shoal with bubbles as it rises, forcing the fish to concentrate, then it lunges, its mouth agape, and gulps its catch.

mouths open – in fact they cannot breathe through their mouths at all, as the food and air passages are totally separate. In most mammals the epiglottis closes the windpipe while food or drink is passing; in cetaceans, the epiglottis reaches right across the throat and plugs directly into the inner end of the nasal passages, effectively sealing off the air system from the digestive system.

Feeding

As anyone who has fallen into water knows, you can get very cold, very quickly, as water conducts heat about 27 times faster than air; under water, further heat loss occurs by swimming. We will lose enough heat to become unconscious after being submerged for only three hours in water at 15°C (59°F) and after only 15 minutes in colder water. Whales, dolphins and seals deal with this problem partly by their layers of insulating blubber, and partly by sheer size – the larger the animal, the smaller its surface area and the lower the heat loss in relation to bodyweight. Large animals lose less heat than small ones, and therefore need less food. So, food is the key, and to reach a large size quickly, young whales take in up to 13 per cent of their bodyweight each day, though this falls to three per cent in adults.

On land, where plants are plentiful, the largest animals are herbivores eating plants at the lowest, most productive, end of the food chain. At sea, plants are less accessible so these large animals are all carnivores. However, the large whales also make use of the bottom productive end of the food chain, the plankton, which is made up of animals and plants that flourish in certain seasons in the year.

These seasonal blooms are most spectacular near the poles where water, cooled by melting ice, sinks to the sea bed and slides on to the ocean floor, while warmer water flows in the opposite direction and wells up to the surface, bringing nutrients. This is particularly noticeable in the southern oceans where the land masses don't cause as much disruption to the currents as in the north. The area of up-welling here is known

as the Antarctic convergence. The long days of summer sun encourage the growth of a bountiful crop of plant plankton, which feeds the animal plankton. 1,000kg (2,200lb) of plant plankton produces 100kg (220lb) of animal plankton, which converts into 10kg (22lb) of whale meat. Each hectare (almost 2½ acres) of Southern Ocean produces over a ton of animal protein a year, which is more than twice the productivity of the best pastureland. In a few short summer months of plenty, many of the great whales grow fast enough to travel and breed right through the winter without necessarily having to feed again.

Baleen whales take advantage of these productive waters using their whalebone filtering apparatus. Their feeding behaviour divides them into two groups, the 'gulpers' and the 'skimmers'. Most of the well known great whales, such as the blue, humpback, fin and minke whales, are 'gulpers'. They are generally called the rorquals, which is the name derived from the Norwegian 'rørhval' that describes the throat grooves or folds on the underside of the mouth. These grooves, or pleats, enable the mouth to stretch and take huge gulps of food-laden water; by then contracting the throat, the water is forced out through the baleen and the sides of the mouth. The 'skimmers', such as the right and bowhead whales, skim along with their mouths open, filtering constantly until enough food has accumulated on the baleen to be scraped off and swallowed. The remaining sei and grey whales do some of both, and will gulp large mouthfuls from the sea bed and also skim food as they are swimming.

The big baleen whales could have been taking as much as 300 million tons of krill from the area of the Antarctic convergence before their numbers were decimated by hunting early in the twentieth century. Since then, other krill eaters such as penguins, seals and the smaller minke whales – which normally eat shoaling fish – have increased in numbers.

There are different sizes and shapes of baleen for various types of food. In the Southern Ocean, the blue whale feeds almost exclusively on krill (*Euphausia superba*), a shrimp-like crustacean about 7.5cm (3in) long that swarms in shoals from a few square metres to several hectares across. In the fin whale, the baleen is finer, making it possible for them to exploit smaller animals such as a krill-like animal called *Thysanoessa* which is half the size of normal krill. Fins also take in large quantities of fish like herring, mackerel and capelin. Humpbacks, which take fish and bottom living animals, have relatively coarse and stiff baleen, as has the grey whale, which feeds almost exclusively on bottom living animals as it swims along, mouth agape, rather like a giant vacuum cleaner. Sei whales have the finest baleen and feed on some of the smallest planktonic crustaceans such as the copepods, as well as fish and krill when available.

As would be expected, the different species of whale are found where their particular food is abundant. Thus blue and fin whales are found where the krill are abundant around the polar oceans in areas of current up-wellings, whereas the sei whale does not go as close to the ice because the smaller plankton, like the copepods, are found in lower latitudes. And right and bowhead whales feed on the smallest plankton nearer the ice edges.

RIGHT River dolphins, such as this Amazon river dolphin, live in murky waters. They use sound to navigate and bristles on their beaks to detect food in the mud. River dolphins also live in the Indus and Ganges in India, the Yangtze in China and La Plata in Argentina.

OPPOSITE A whale's blow hole is surrounded by thick muscular lips which keep it closed tight underwater. In baleen whales there are two blow holes lying behind a raised ridge or cutwater which prevents their being flooded during breathing.

Teeth

Most whales and dolphins have teeth. The teeth are simple pegs with a root and a crown though the numbers vary from two to 200, depending on the type of food that is eaten.

The toothed whales are hunters and different types of food call for different types and sizes of teeth. Oceanic dolphins eat fish and squid and their long beaks with many small sharp teeth are well suited for grasping small, slippery prey. Porpoises have chisel shaped teeth for eating relatively large smooth fish. River dolphins have flattened molar-like teeth for eating the armoured catfish found on muddy river beds. Those that

specialise in eating squid presumably just need to grab their food, stop it escaping and then eat their prey whole. These whales have few teeth in the front of both jaws, such as the pilot whales, or they have one or two pairs of teeth on their lower jaws such as the beaked whales.

Sperm whales are the largest toothed whale with males reaching 19m (62ft) and females about 13m (42ft). They only

BELOW Like many land mammals where males and females remain apart except when mating, dolphin groups include nurseries of females and young, and separate bachelor groups.

LEFT Sperm whales appear to have a matriarchal society where the fundamental unit is the nursery group of between 10 and 20 mothers, and young and immature calves of both sexes. In autumn this group is joined by fully grown mature males returning from polar feeding grounds. The females are at the centre of sexual activity, and males fight for, and defend, the position of dominant male. Rival males threaten each other with tail slaps, breaching and explosive claps of their jaws, and may butt, bite, or rake each other with their teeth; the prize is the possession of the harem for the season. Usually there is only one large adult male in the harem herd, though he may sometimes tolerate the presence of one or two subordinate males.

have teeth in the lower jaw and in fact manage perfectly well without teeth until they are 10 years old. This whale is probably one of the easiest to recognise because of its large box-like head that is about one-third of the body length that may overhang the relatively puny bottom jaw by up to 1.5m (5ft).

Sperm whales dive to catch their food, which is mainly giant squid that live in depths of 1,000m (3,300ft) or more. Their skin often has round scar marks that most likely result from struggles with giant squid in the deep ocean. These whales are the greatest divers and regularly dive to over 1,200m (4,000ft) and can remain down for up to an hour. One caught off South Africa spent almost two hours underwater before it was caught. Even deeper dives may be made as bottom-living sharks have been found in the stomachs of these whales where the sea-bed is deeper than 3,000m (9,000ft). On its return to the surface, the first exhalation can often sound like an explosion that can be heard some distance away.

As most cetaceans swallow their food whole, they don't have the powerful jaw muscles or moveable tongues found in land mammals. Some toothed whales, like Orcas, sometimes called the killer whale, can move the tips of their tongue, but in baleen whales it is no more than a massive muscle covering the bottom of the mouth. The tongue of an adult blue whale can weigh as much as a full-grown elephant.

Social Communities

On land, it is relatively easy to define herds of animals living within a particular area. But in the sea, for us to define areas and schools of whales is more difficult, with our limited land-based senses: to us, a whale may appear to be travelling alone, but in fact it could well be part of a social unit whose members are out of our sight, but not beyond the whale's own hearing. Generally baleen whales tend to form loose communities, but at certain seasons they come together into more closely knit breeding groups that are involved in intense social activity. Carnivores have most to gain from the development of cooperation and social assistance, because it is helpful when hunting. The toothed whales show a complete range of social structure, from the solitary beaked whales to the oceanic dolphins that may form communities of thousands, although most of the coastal dolphins, porpoises and pilot whales form smaller groups of between six and sixty individuals.

These whales, like dolphins, have rigid social hierarchies where the formal organization is made clear by various threat

behaviours. There is often a formal vertical pattern, with the most dominant animal nearest the surface and the most subordinate at the deepest level. When on the move, groups of dolphins often adopt particular formations. Thus a wedge shape has the most experienced and dominant animals in the lead, and younger animals protected in the centre. Other formations include open squares, hollow circles or single files. When feeding, these formations break down, but there are still well defined roles, as they usually cooperate to catch food, often with the dominant animals taking first bite, followed by others. Bottlenose dolphins have been seen herding shoals of fish, or corralling them like sheepdogs, while the rest of the group takes turns in feeding.

Orcas are particularly astute, and remain in contact with each other throughout a hunt, and by signal or demonstration modify their behaviour to take advantage of changes in the situation; they even organize themselves into respiratory units, which ensures that no member is ever breathing alone. Family groups may remain intact for life, and members learn to work together to herd salmon or tilt ice floes to tip seals into the water, as well as joining forces to bring down grey whale calves.

The Songs of the Whales

Seafaring literature is full of stories of mysterious sounds at sea. In the days of sail it was possible to hear every creak and groan of a ship's timbers and sails, and in the quiet of the night, calls and songs could be heard, many of which probably led to stories of haunted ships and singing sirens. Ancient mariners had known for years that it was possible to track cetaceans by their characteristic songs, and the nineteenth-century whalers could distinguish between right whales, humpbacks, greys, belugas and pilot whales.

As sound travels four times faster through water than through the air, all marine mammals have developed the use of sound to communicate. Some animals are able to 'talk' to each other over large distances, although engine noises and seismic explosions such as are used in oil exploration can greatly reduce their capacity to hear each other. Sound is also used for navigation and, in a similar way to bats, a sound is emitted and the echo received. This echo location tells the animal about its surroundings and, in some cases, whether an object is soft or hard. Unlike the sound made by bats, which cannot be heard by the human ear, most whale sounds can be heard. Some dolphins use sound to catch food, producing a noise of such intensity that they can stun or even kill fish at close range.

All whales and dolphins make a wide range of sounds. Some of the most powerful sounds come from the baleen whales: fin whales produce a low-frequency moan; right whales, grey and minke whales produce short thumps or knocks; various chirps and whistles seem to be produced by

ABOVE TOP Whale songs provide a whole range of information. Humpback whales' songs are the most well researched. Their songs can tell the listener – including humans – information about who and where the whales are, the number in the group, the reproductive state, food availability and presence of predators.

ABOVE The skull and upper jaw in dolphins are hollow on top, giving a concave surface on which rests the melon. Sound waves produced in the nasal passages are possibly reflected off the curved bone of the head and focussed into a beam by the lens-shaped melon.

LEFT The intelligence of cetaceans is the subject of ongoing debate. But it is clear, from years of experience from those working with dolphins that they are not only intelligent or 'clever', but they demonstrate a clear conscious awareness. In many cases, they have had beneficial therapeutic effects for humans, for example, dolphins have been reported to aid children with autism.

most baleen whales; and high-frequency clicks that last less than a hundredth of a second have been recorded for grey, fin, sei, tropical and humpback whales. The thumps of the minke whale, the moans of fin whales and the whistles of humpback whales are all produced with such distinctive frequencies and repetition rates that individuals can be recognized over great distances. A blue whale's whistle, recorded at 188 decibels, is the loudest sound to be produced by any animal, and, with a power exceeding even that of a passing jet plane (usually about 140 – 170 decibels), will travel long distances under water. Even the relatively small minke whale has a song recorded at 152 decibels. Acoustic scans employed by blue and minke whales seem to use frequencies that correlate well with the sizes of their favoured food prey; and the reverberations of the moans produced by fin whales may be great enough to span an entire ocean. Humpbacks produce themes or songs that can last up to 30 minutes, and may be the most complex in the animal kingdom. A ritual collection of songs separated by brief pauses can last more than 24 hours.

The distance that a sound travels depends on its wavelength or frequency, so that high-pitched sounds travel a fraction of the distance of low-pitched sounds. Hence long-range communication uses low frequencies, like the trans-oceanic moans of the fin whale. These low frequencies have long wavelengths, and the moans of the fin whale have wavelengths of about 75m (245ft) which will pass over most obstacles and only bounce back from large objects like an oil tanker or submarine bank. Such long wavelength sounds have limited use in navigation, but clearly the long migrations of the great

baleen whales has led to their favouring of long-range communication.

The speed with which sound travels in water also changes with temperature and pressure. As you go deeper, the speed decreases until you reach a band of water of higher temperature, which in polar waters may occur near the surface, but in warmer areas may be as deep as 1,100m (3,610ft). In these bands of higher water temperature, called the thermocline, the speed of sound increases, and it can be heard over a long distance without much sound loss. Whales can communicate over huge distances by emitting their sounds within this deeper band of water.

It is the toothed whales, such as the dolphins, which have highly developed their sounds for echo location with some being able to distinguish nets in water where the visibility is virtually zero. They produce a steady stream of intense clicks that can vary in rate up to 1,000 per second to build an accurate echo picture. Their sonar system uses lower frequencies for communication, and higher ones for navigation and even hunting. Some can produce two different frequencies simultaneously and the most efficient can flatten or heighten the beam of sound in order to focus on a target. All achieve greater acuity by scanning or sweeping their sonar beams over the target with movements of their heads or bodies as they listen. Belugas are called 'canaries of the sea' because of the songs they produce. The river dolphins can produce ultrasonic sounds similar to those produced by bats. They are able to 'see' in the murky river waters where eyes are basically useless. Many toothed whales communicate directly with each other by

clear whistles, which not only vary from species to species, but seem to be personal to each individual. The frequency and intensity of conversations by whistle increases when animals assemble to hunt.

Cetaceans do not produce sounds the same way as land animals as no air escapes from the blow hole. Sound is produced either by vibration of the larynx or of the nasal plugs. Alternatively, air can be channelled through tubes between air pockets within the head; muscles constrict air passages, producing a vibration - rather like squeezing the neck of an inflated balloon produces sound.

Nor do cetaceans hear like land animals. While their ancestors probably had normal external ears designed for airborne sounds, in water these became redundant and reduced to pinholes plugged with wax, and the sound is picked up through the bones of the skull or jaw. Just as the melon projects the sound forward, so it, and the extra fat channels through the jaws, conducts the sound directly to the inner ears. The system is so sensitive that a dolphin in a large tank can hear a teaspoonful of water being poured in anywhere.

Intelligence

No-one can fail to be in awe of the ability of cetaceans to imitate, learn and communicate and studies generally conclude that their relative intelligence is somewhere between that of a dog and a chimpanzee. But this is not the full story as those working with dolphins, and those with experience of their therapeutic effects, demonstrate that the animals have a conscious awareness. So-called intelligence tests bear little resemblance to the natural world of dolphins and it is likely that they could rapidly get bored with repeated meaningless tasks. Under similar conditions, humans are less adept than pigeons!

Measuring intelligence is difficult and can only be relative. Comparing brain sizes tells us something about capacity but little about intelligence. The fact is that there are large differences in the demands made on the brain and consequently in the development of different areas. Cetaceans live in an environment where sound and touch are most important, so the relevant parts of the brain are the best developed.

Our brain structure is similar to dolphins, but our best areas of development are those associated with motor skills made possible by our hands, while cetaceans seem to concentrate on social perception. It is perhaps sufficient to note that we are different creatures with different priorities and strengths and

BELOW Fortunately, strandings are rare events, but whether navigational error or confusion is the cause, the sight of these beautiful animals, stranded helplessly out of their normal environment, is surely among the most tragic.

weaknesses. However, it should be recognized that cetaceans probably have mental experiences that have important effects on their behaviour.

Whales and dolphins also play, with some groups spending more time playing with toys such as feathers than feeding, and stones can become the focus of long and intricate games. In the animal kingdom, play is usually a functional behaviour as a preparation for adult life. Cetaceans spend much time in play, but this is often not restricted to young as in many species adults also play much of the time.

Strandings

Cetaceans are clearly well adapted to their environment, but despite their obvious abilities, some still get into trouble: ships occasionally collide with whales, and there have been cases where apparently a whale has fatally attacked a ship. Some hunted whales did not learn to avoid ships and even approached vessels, to their misfortune. In human terms, this does not seem very clever.

Occasionally apparently healthy individuals or sometimes whole families of whales or dolphins will beach themselves. Some old, but largely discounted, explanations held that the animals were dying and wanted to commit suicide or that some ancestral drive made them want to return to land.

Orcas may be left stranded after chasing seals or penguins, or schools may panic when being attacked or when finding themselves in shallow water. There are some places where, for centuries, whales have been known to strand themselves. These could be just difficult areas to navigate such as those places having a gently sloping sea floor which does not give a clear echo. Disorientation could be caused by the weather or a change in the character of the water or by infections such as parasites in the inner ear. Whatever the cause, once an animal finds itself in trouble it cries for help. Its companions come to its aid, but they too get into trouble with the end result that the whole group can be left high and dry. This also explains why, once an individual has been towed away, it will immediately return to help its companions.

Comforting and Succouring Behaviours

Obviously, for these air-breathing mammals, the most serious problems arise when something happens which makes it difficult or impossible to swim. A minor injury or concussion from which a land animal can recover can be fatal for a whale. So it is not surprising that most whales and dolphins come to the aid of others in distress and that this behaviour pattern involves the simple response of helping an ailing animal to get to the surface to breathe. This is most common in females that assist birthing mothers to bring their new-born to the surface, but it also extends to any individual in difficulty.

The fact that cetaceans will stand by a stranded or injured animal was recorded by Aristotle and was well-known to old whalers, who called it 'heaving to' or 'bringing to a slow'. Whalers knew that a securely harpooned, but not badly

injured, whale was the best possible lure for enticing others within range, and used it to capture whole groups of sperm whales. There are also records of more active behaviour in these situations, such as harpoon lines being bitten and boats crushed by the bystanders, or animals putting themselves between the attacking boat and the injured individual.

When in trouble, they summon help with a distress call and often come to the aid of individuals that were out of sight. But help can be given without calling and supporting behaviour can be initiated by the struggle or laboured breathing of a drowning animal. In one record, a diver in the Caribbean was repeatedly 'rescued' by a group of false killer whales every time they heard him breathing through a waterlogged snorkel.

Breeding

Female baleen whales are usually larger than males, and vice versa in toothed whales, but otherwise there are few obvious differences between whale sexes. This makes behaviour and sound key in sexual activity, as witnessed in the elaborate songs of humpback whales. It is even possible that some cetaceans can 'see' different sexes with their echo location.

All cetaceans have an elaborate courtship behaviour. There

ABOVE The mother usually turns on her side to feed her calf, giving easier access to her nipples which, under pressure from the milk, protrude from their mammary slits. Suckling is done between breaths under water, which is helped by the mother forcing out the rich milk which is about 40 per cent fat (compared to two per cent in human milk). Large baleen whales produce up to 600 litres (132 gallons) of milk a day and the calves double their weight in the first week. Weaning takes place when the calves are more than half grown and feeding on their own.

OPPOSITE Narwhal males are easily distinguished from females because of their long tusk which is used in aggressive encounters between males, but it is not known if it has any other function. When Narwhals fight, their tusks make a 'clacking' sound, like two musical sticks hitting together. They usually do not injure each other in these disputes, but in some other species such as the beaked whales and some of the dolphins, the bulls all bear scars which are testament to battles between male rivals.

is the lunging display of the Humpback whale, and the resounding head-on collision of the shortfin pilot whales, but mostly the preliminaries to mating involve long and gentle mutual caressing. A lot of time is spent in sexual activity. Dolphins engage in love-play with almost any creature in sight as well as with family members. Gregarious species are always touching and teasing each other in ways that are obviously sexually stimulating, but true foreplay involves much more intense nuzzling, nibbling, rubbing and stroking. This ends when one or both adopt specific pre-mating postures. For example, the bottlenose dolphin male throws his body into a sinuous s-shaped curve.

The greatest difference between the sexes is shown by the Narwhal, which lives in the icy waters of the north above the Arctic circle to the edge of the ice pack around the Greenland Sea and in the Davis Strait, between Canada and Greenland. They are often found in the ice pack sheltering from Orcas and polar bears in small areas of open water. Their most distinctive physical feature is their teeth. The upper jaw has two teeth that in the females are usually embedded in the gum, leaving them basically toothless. In males, the tusk is actually the left tooth that grows out through the gum at the front of the jaw to form a straight, tapered, spiral tusk up to 3m (9ft) long. Occasionally females develop a tusk, and a few animals of either sex can have two tusks. In times before the narwhal species was widely known about, their tusks were sold as unicorn horns in Europe!

Birth is a difficult time for cetaceans. The young are born tail-first, a clear advantage if you breathe air and are born underwater. Often, there are other animals behaving like midwives or aunts to assist and protect the young and mother. The process may take some time with only the tail protruding, sometimes for hours, but the last part of the birth happens quickly and the newborn calf, with no air in its lungs, tends to sink, but is helped to the surface by the mother and other midwives within seconds. Contact with the air initiates breathing and the calf takes its first breath and then swims very close to the mother. The instinctive behaviour of pushing the young to the surface persists even if the calf is stillborn, which may partly explain why some people have been saved from drowning by dolphins and why some cetaceans can often be seen playing with objects like lumps of wood on the surface.

BELOW Dolphins, as in all cetaceans, have elaborate courtships, but dolphins in particular are well known for their touching and caressing play that can often be sexual and end up in mating, like in these spinner dolphins, *Stenella longirostris*.

Seals

Like the whales and dolphins, seals have mastered the art of living and feeding in the sea, but unlike the cetaceans, they need to return to land or ice in order to mate, rest, give birth and moult.

ABOVE The 33 seal species, except monk seals, are mainly found in cool polar and temperate waters, only living in warmer areas that are washed by cooler currents. These California sea lions are found on the western coast of North America.

All seals are in a group called Pinnipeds, a name which comes from the Latin words 'pinna' meaning a 'fin' or 'wing' and 'pedis' meaning 'foot'. Like whales and dolphins, seals evolved from land mammals and are descended from either bear-like or otter-like creatures that entered the seas millions of years ago. Seals generally have few predators, the main ones being orcas, some sharks, polar bears and man.

Living in colder waters, seals have evolved some of the same adaptations as whales. Layers of blubber under the skin protect them from the cold and help give them their streamlined torpedo-shape for fast swimming underwater. Their blood is able to store large amounts of oxygen for deep and prolonged dives – dives of up to 1,600m (over 5,000ft) and two hours having been recorded.

With the sole exception of the walrus, which is in a group of its own, all seals are divided into two groups with the most obvious visible difference being whether or not there is an external ear flap.

The eared seals include sea lions and fur seals. Fur seals have a pointed snout and long hairs that cover a thick under-fur: in the past, this fur was of considerable commercial value which, in many cases, resulted in a severe depletion of numbers due to hunting. They have large front and back flippers which have no fur; the front ones can be turned outward for support and the rear can be turned forward underneath the body for movement on land. They walk using both their hind and fore flippers, and they swim using a sculling movement of their front flippers. The performing seals in captivity are usually sea lions which have a blunt snout and a coat of short coarse hairs covering a small amount of under-fur.

The rest are the true seals which do not have an external ear flap and include the northern seals, like the grey, the Antarctic seals, the monk seals - the only group that lives in tropical waters - and the hooded and elephant seals. The flippers of these seals are covered in fur, though this is difficult to see when the animals are wet. They are not as agile on land as their eared cousins and they drag themselves along using their front flippers or bodies. They have relatively small front flippers, which are used as rudders for steering underwater, their hind flippers providing the propulsion.

The walrus, in a family of its own, has some characteristics of both eared and true seals. The most notable feature is their long tusks, which are enlarged canine teeth weighing more than 5kg (11lb) and growing up to 1m (3ft) long. They are formidable and used in threat displays and fighting, but also help the walrus haul itself out onto the ice. They are impressive animals, with a skin up to 6cm (2½in) thick, a body length of 3m (almost 10ft) in length and weight, on average, of between 1,200 – 1,500kg (2,640 – 3,300lb). At this size they have few enemies, excluding humans, although calves are preyed upon by polar bears and orcas. The Atlantic walrus is found around the Arctic ocean from northern Canada eastwards to the Kara Sea; its Pacific cousin occurs from the East Siberian Sea to Alaska as well as off the north coast of central Russia.

Walrus were hunted extensively in the past and their numbers were decimated. They have yet to show significant signs of recovery because they breed slowly and can live for up to 40 years. Although they do haul themselves out onto land, they prefer to use first-year ice with open leads or areas of open water, so they tend to follow the ice edge. In summer, as the ice retreats northwards, males and females move to separate feeding areas.

Courtship and mating take place between January and April when adult males make a number of taps, knocks, pulses and bell sounds under the water to attract females and demonstrate a superiority over other males and although mature at between 6 and 10 years, they usually do not compete and mate successfully until about 15 years old.

True Seals

The true seals mainly live in the colder parts of the world and make their homes in both the Antarctic and Arctic. In and around Antarctica, the ice specialists are the leopard, the Weddell, the crab-eater and the Ross seals, while their long-distance Arctic relatives are the harp, hooded, ribbon, ringed, spotted and bearded seals.

Unlike the other Antarctic seal species that prefer the ice edge, Weddell seals prefer to stay on the pack ice around the

BELOW Seals living among the ice migrate north and south with the seasonal shifting of the ice-edge. They hunt beneath the ice and keep breathing holes open by biting away ice. Weddell seals are able to return to their air hole after travelling almost 3km (2 miles) away in search of food.

RIGHT The ice-breeding harp seal is found in waters of the Arctic and the far north Atlantic Oceans. The pups are born with a yellowish fur, called a 'yellow-coat' which turns white after a couple of days, producing the 'white-coat' pup.

Antarctic continent, although there are small populations that breed on some of the Antarctic islands such as South Georgia, the South Sandwich Islands, the South Shetland Islands and the South Orkney Islands. All seals are vocal, but the underwater calls of the Weddell seals can be heard through the ice by a listener on the surface. Video cameras attached to seals show that they are stealth hunters, approaching within centimetres of cod without startling the fish, and that they do not appear to use sound to hunt, relying instead on their acute underwater vision and often using the under-ice surface for backlighting. The seals have also been observed flushing out smaller fish by blowing air into sub-ice crevices. Weddell seals are excellent divers, and feeding dives to depths of 200 – 400m (650 – 1,300ft) for periods of up to 15 minutes are common.

Maintaining the breathing hole is vital for air, but it also presents a danger: in the Arctic, polar bears, with their extraordinary sense of hearing and smell, can detect the presence of breathing holes and seals beneath the ice. The bears have infinite patience, and wait tirelessly by these holes for the seal to break surface.

Breeding

Seals give birth on land or ice. Usually adult males or bulls gather harems of females, or cows. The young is a pup that grows until four or five months old, when it becomes a yearling, although young walrus are known as calves. Sealers used to call breeding males 'wigs' and females 'clapmatches'. Harp seals are probably the most well known due to the history of seal hunting. Like most mating seals, during the breeding season, which takes place on the pack ice from February to March, they gather together in large groups which may contain up to 2,000 seals per square kilometre (½ a square mile).

Seals moult periodically and for some, like the harp seal, hunters have named each growth phase. The pups are born with a yellowish fur, called a 'yellow-coat' which turns white after a couple of days, producing the 'white-coat' pup. After a couple of weeks the white coat moults, leaving tufts of white fur which is called a 'ragged-jacket', but by 4 weeks the white fur has moulted completely, and at this stage it is called a 'beater'. The juvenile coat, from about 14 months until maturity at four or more years, has larger spots and the young seal is now called a 'bedlamer' which is a corruption of 'bête de la mer', the name given to the seals in the 15th and 16th centuries by Breton settlers in Canada. The adults are silvery grey coloured, with a horse-shoe or harp shaped pattern on their backs.

After breeding and moulting, harp seals disperse widely into Arctic and sub-Arctic waters to feed during the summer and autumn. In late September, ahead of the advancing ice, nearly all of the adults and most of the juveniles move south to their winter breeding grounds although many of the juveniles and a few non-breeding adults stay in the north all year round.

Hooded seals, named for the inflatable crest or hood on the adult male's forehead, have also been given other names as a result of their fur. They give birth on drifting pack ice and the juveniles, less than 14 months old, are called 'blue-backs': at this stage in their development their pelt was greatly valued.

LEFT The Atlantic grey seal, a true seal living on both coasts of the Atlantic, doesn't migrate but disperses to sea after breeding. They have never been commercially hunted, but the fishing industry has called for culls, blaming the seals for declining fish catches, although intensive fishing is the major cause of reduced fish stocks.

BELOW Monk seals, such as this Mediterranean monk seal, are endangered. Ancient Greeks held that their skins gave protection against lightning and gout and a flipper under the pillow gave relief from insomnia! Today the greatest threats are entanglement in fishing gear and disturbance. They are very sensitive to disturbance, a serious problem in their densely populated habitat.

OPPOSITE Bearded seals are a polar bear's major food; they are solitary and found in areas of broken pack ice and in shorefast ice where they maintain breathing holes. Because of the threat from polar bears, bearded seal pups grow quickly and can swim and dive within the first week. Nursing lasts18 to 24 days, they quickly put on weight and moult into the adult coat as they are weaned.

Leopard seals, so-named because of their spotted coat, are the largest of the Antarctic seals, achieving sexual maturity at between two and seven years. During the mating season they give out soft lyrical calls. They give birth on ice floes and there is a short suckling period of about a month. The pups, with a soft thick, grey coloured coat, are initially about 1.5m (5ft) long and weigh 35kg (80lb); however, they put on weight and protective blubber very quickly.

Feeding

A seal's diet consists of a wide variety of food, ranging from krill in the Southern Ocean through crustaceans and shellfish to fish and squid. The walrus, which live in shallow continental waters usually less than 100m (330ft) deep, feed on animals living in or on the sea bed such as clams, when they are available; but they will also take snails, sea cucumbers, crabs and shrimps and even, occasionally, fish and seals. In murky waters the stiff whiskers around the snout are used to find food, and the seal can do this even in the total darkness of the northern Arctic winter. It digs out the food from the sediment using its snout and squirts a jet of water or waves its front flippers to clear away the silt.

Leopard seals eat a large variety of food, using their wide, gaping mouths and massive jaws most effectively. During winter their most important food is krill, but they also eat squid, fish and other seals, especially newly weaned crab-eater seals during December and January. Some specialize in eating penguins when these are available in late January and

February. Their large fore-flippers, which are unusually long for a 'true' seal, allow them great speed and manoeuvrability in the water.

The least well known and rarest of the Antarctic seals is the Ross seal, named after the British explorer who obtained the first specimen. It is mostly found on the pack ice around the

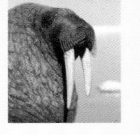

the Antarctic continent, and, unlike other, more gregarious seals, they tend to be more isolated and widely spread out – two key reasons why this seal is least well known.

By contrast, crab-eaters are the most numerous seals in the world, with some population estimates of around 15 million, although it may be less. They are found throughout the pack ice around Antarctica, mostly around the edge of the ice. Their name is curious, as their major food is Antarctic krill and not crabs. Like most seals that live on and around the ice edge, crab-eaters are dependent on the seasonal movement of the ice, travelling long distances around the Southern Ocean and near sub-Antarctic islands, and they have even been found in South Africa, South America, New Zealand and Australia. They have special lobed teeth that sieve the krill out of the water. Crab-eater seal pups and juveniles are heavily preyed on by leopard seals, especially newly weaned pups during the spring and summer, and this predation is a key influence on the lifestyle and habits of the species.

The ringed seal is another Arctic seal which has several different sub-species named after the places they're found. The Arctic ringed seal is found throughout the Arctic Ocean and the Bering Sea, ranging as far south as Newfoundland and northern Norway. There is also an Okhotsk Sea ringed seal, a Baltic ringed seal and around 2,000 Ladoga ringed seals found in Lake Ladoga in western Russia, but only about 220 – 250 Saimaa seals remain in Lake Saimaa in eastern Finland. The retreat of ice during the last glaciation caused the Baltic ringed

seal to become separated from the Arctic ringed seal about 11,000 years ago, and also caused the Saimaa and Ladoga seals to be trapped in their respective freshwater lakes about 8,000–9,000 years ago.

Bearded seals are a major food for polar bears. Unlike most seals they are solitary and found in seasonally ice-covered waters less than 200m (500ft) deep. They prefer to inhabit areas of broken pack ice and drifting ice floes, but are quite versatile and also occur in areas of shorefast ice and thick ice where they are able to maintain breathing holes. Many of the seals move long distances to follow the receding ice in the summer. The threat from Polar bears has lead the bearded seal pups to have one of the quickest growths. Pupping and moulting take place on the ice before mid-March to early May. The pups have one of the quickest developments, with nursing lasting only 18 – 24 days; they quickly put on weight and moult into the adult coat at the same time as they are weaned. They learn to swim very shortly after being born, and at less than a week old have been recorded diving for more than 5 minutes to as deep as 75m (250ft).

Eared Seals

Although many of the eared seals are found near the Antarctic and Arctic regions, they tend to live much further away from the ice in the more cool temperate regions and are much more comfortable on land than the true seals. California sea lions are probably the best known. These agile seals can reach

2m (6ft) in length and feed mainly on fish, squid and octopus and live mostly along the west coast of North America from Vancouver Island in the north to Tres Marias Islands, off Mexico, in the south. Similar sea lions are found in the Galapagos Islands; and in the southern Sea of Japan there are other species, such as the South American and Australian sea lions and the New Zealand, or Hooker's, sea lion.

Eared seals haul out on their preferred beaches to mate and moult and sometimes the adult male or bull gathers a harem of cows. In some species the bull must establish a territory, fighting off challenges from rivals. Before this happens, the females will usually already be on the beach where they will give birth to pups conceived during the previous breeding season. A short time after birth – sometimes two weeks – the males mate with the females. But the fertilised egg is held for two or three months before it is implanted in the womb. This ensures that the pregnancy starts at the right time so that the pups can be born during the correct season and in the right place.

Elephant seals, so named because of their long elephant-like noses, are renowned for long migrations and deep diving abilities. They are the largest seals with males reaching up to 4.5m (14½ft) and weighing 2,300kg (over 5,000lb), which is up to seven times more than females. Northern Elephant seals give birth and moult in California and Baja California, mostly on

ABOVE Northern elephant seals congregate onshore during the breeding season, the moult season, and the juvenile haul-out period in the autumn. Breeding takes place from December until March with adult males first arriving to fight for dominance to gain access to the females. The pups, resulting from the previous year's mating, are born between 2 and 7 days in January after the mother has arrived. Different sexes and ages moult at different times and the fur tends to come off in sheets.

offshore islands. Outside the breeding and moulting seasons they feed as far north as the Gulf of Alaska.

These seals were hunted for their blubber and oil in the 19th century. At one point there were only 100 – 1,000 northern elephant seals left on the Mexican Isla de Guadalupe, but following protection early in the 20th century they have made a remarkable recovery.

Monk seals live in warmer areas. There were three species: the Caribbean, Hawaiian and Mediterranean, but the Caribbean seal is now extinct and the remaining two are the most endangered seals. Formerly found all over the Mediterranean Sea, Black Sea and northwest African coast, there are now fewer than 400 Mediterranean monk seals. Hawaiian monk seals, which mostly inhabit the north western Hawaiian Islands, fare little better. A key reason for their decline is disturbance by military and coastguard activities and tourism.

And Finally ...
The Mermaids!

Legends of mermaids are well known. And it is thought that one group of mammals, the dugongs and manatees, because they recline in a semi-upright position when suckling their young, could be one origin of these ancient stories.

These animals belong to a group called the Sirenia, after the mythological sirens or sea nymphs that lured sailors onto rocks with their songs. They actually look nothing like the mermaids of literature, but are believed to have reached their present stage of evolution after 50 million years or more and share ancestry with the elephant.

Manatees and dugongs are large, gentle giants, spending their lives in the water and are entirely vegetarian, eating up to 10 kg (22lb) of seagrass a day. They grow to over four metres (13ft) and can weigh up to 1,500kg (3,300lb). Manatees have paddle-shaped tails and dugongs have a tail that is pointed on the ends like a whale's. Both use their tails to move through the water and their two front limbs are for steering and scooping up food. They have small eyes, yet they can see fairly well, and they have no external ears, but they hear very well.

Dugongs reproduce slowly, and if food is short they give up breeding altogether. Their food is becoming in very short supply as in much of the tropics seagrass beds are being cleared for shrimp farms and salt pans, or being smothered by silt and mud pouring off the land due to deforestation or intensive farming.

The dugongs' traditional haunts are the coastal seagrasses and mangrove swamps of the tropics, from East Africa to Vanuatu and northern Australia, in the South Pacific. But today there are only small populations in a few areas as their habitat is being severely reduced.

LEFT The north American manatee lives in the coastal waters of the south eastern US, especially Florida and the Caribbean, and the north eastern coast of South America. The rare south American manatee prefers the still waters of the Amazon. The west African manatee can be found from Senegal to Angola.

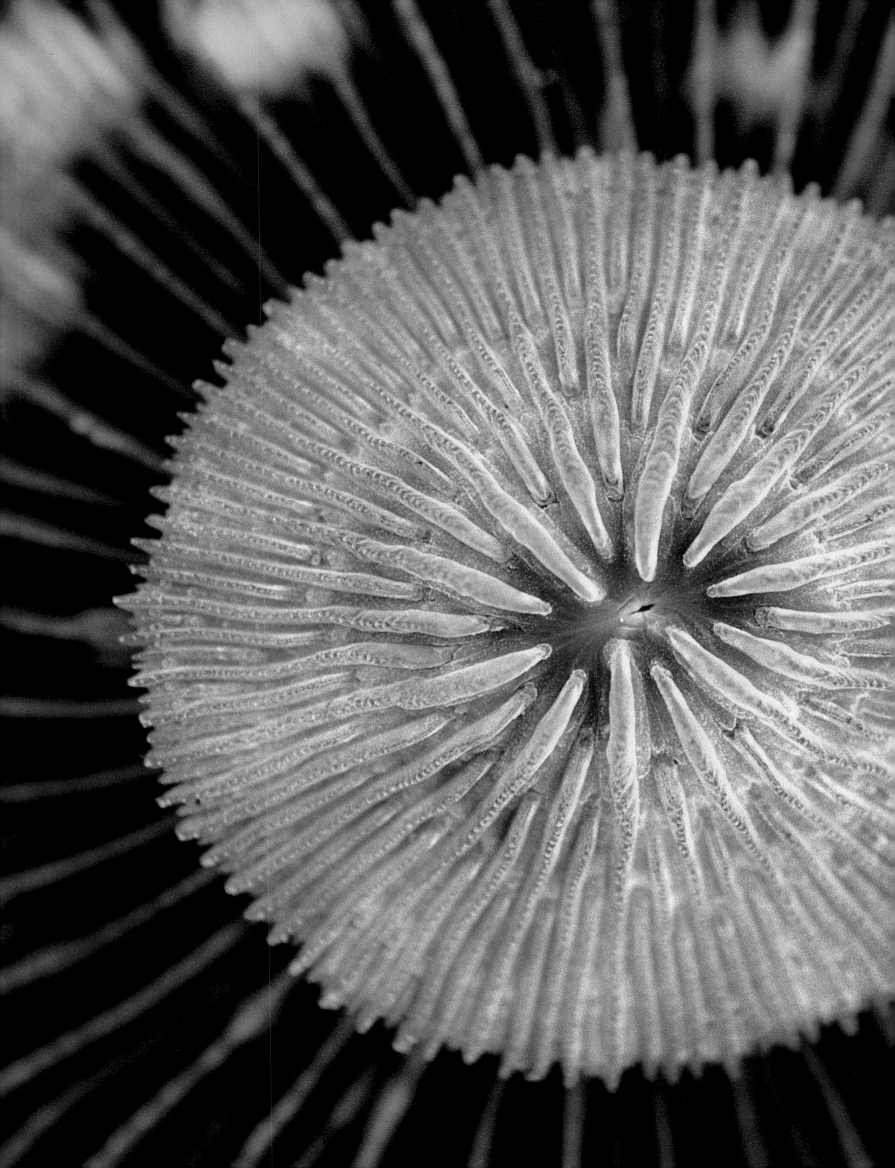

CHAPTER SIX

LIVING LIGHT

While sailing a little south of the Plata on one very dark night the sea presented a wonderful spectacle. There was a fresh breeze, and every part of the surface, which during the day is seen as foam, now glowed with a pale light. The vessel drove before her bows billions of liquid phosphorus, and in her wake she was followed by a milky train. As far as the eye reached, the crest of every wave was bright, and the sky above the horizon from the reflected glare of these vivid flames, was not so utterly obscure as over the vault of the heavens.

Charles Darwin, HMS Beagle, December 1833

Such was the description of bioluminescence by Charles Darwin on his famous voyage. But the spectacle of which he writes is still a regular occurrence today, and one that even now engenders the same feeling of wonder. So, let us look into the dark oceans a little closer at this living light…

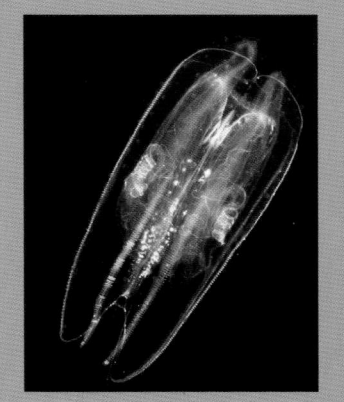

The use of light by animals, and sometimes plants, is well known. Bioluminescence – literally 'living light' – is sometimes called phosphorescence (shown here by a mushroom coral). It is probably one of the strangest phenomena of the ocean world.

Lights in the Darkness

Although little daylight reaches the dim regions below 1,500m (5,000ft), this does not mean that the animals here live in total darkness. There is much local illumination in the form of flashes or even of continuous light – illumination that emanates from the animals themselves.

In the 7th century, bioluminescence was thought to be caused by the sea absorbing the sun by day and emitting it at night. Another view was that the flashes were caused by friction between waves, or between the waves and an object such as the side of a ship. In the mid-eighteenth century, Benjamin Franklin thought that it was an electrical discharge between salt and water particles. But later in the same year that Franklin proposed this theory, two Venetian naturalists proved that bioluminescence in the Adriatic was caused by the single-celled animal *Noctiluca*, the name literally meaning 'night light'. Some time later another naturalist observed bioluminescence in the Mediterranean jellyfish, *Pelagia noctiluca* – although this just confirmed earlier reports by the Roman naturalist, Pliny.

Deep-sea researchers who have explored these regions have described a variety of light-producing animals, including squid, prawns and many fish. Most of the starfish from the seabed are also luminescent. In fact about three-quarters of all animals that swim freely at depths of 150 – 1,500m (500 – 5,000ft) are able to produce light in their own bodies. The most luminous depth seems to be at about 600m (2,000ft), but flashes from living organisms have been recorded as deep as 3,000m (10,000ft). In the deeper oceans there are angler fish with light lures, lantern fish and squid with light spots on their underside, as well as smaller luminescent planktonic creatures. On the sea surface at night, displays of light can take on fantastic forms, from spinning wheels to streaks of light stretching into the distance.

Today it is common knowledge that many organisms can produce light. On land there are fireflies, glow-worms and even luminescent mushrooms; but in the sea, a much larger number of animals are able to use and produce some form of light. There are many different types of bioluminescent displays, according to the reasons for the light and the way it is produced. It also rather depends on the observer: for instance, the apparent intensity will depend on how long the observer has been in the dark; and the perception of colour differs between individuals. However, the large number of observations and recordings over the years, coming mainly from seafarers who have sailed the seven seas for centuries, has enabled different types of bioluminescence to be identified. Seafarers continue today to provide descriptions of spectacular bioluminescent displays at sea.

LEFT Ctenophores, or sea gooseberries, can generate their own light, but the reflection of external light from their beating hairs or comb-rows is, nonetheless, spectacular.

OPPOSITE The luminescent jelly fish, *Pelagia noctiluca*, found in the Mediterranean, was one of the first animals discovered to produce its own luminescence as opposed to any mechanical or physical phenomenon. The purple patches on the animals are the light producing areas that are also concentrated around the rim.

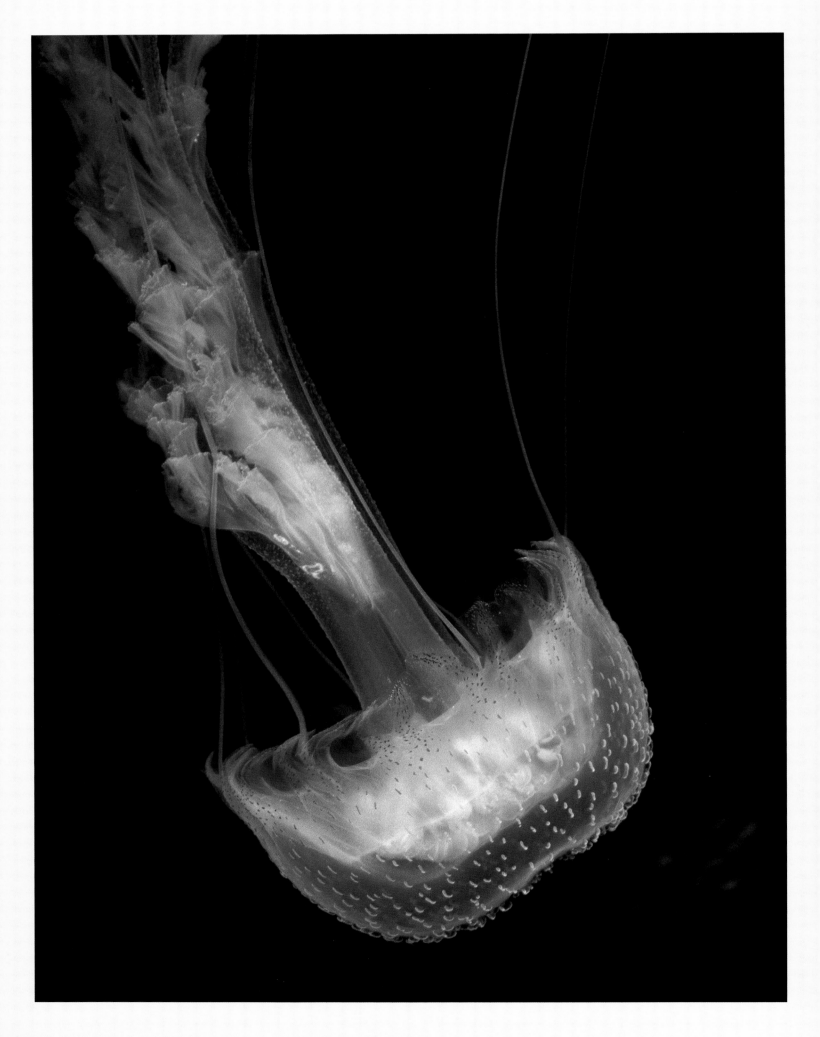

Milky Sea or White Water

Several seafarers have often referred to a ghostly white appearance of the sea. This is usually an even, diffuse glow in, or immediately beneath, the surface water that extends over a large distance. There are no distinct shapes, and the glow is not affected by mechanical disturbances such as the wake of a passing ship. Milky sea is commonly recorded between July and September in the Arabian Sea and Malacca Straits, but it has been recorded elsewhere and at other times of the year. Normally there is a definite edge to the area, although the wind may blow the luminescence into slicks or streaks across the water. Some seafarers have noted a change in the sea temperature that is probably an indication that the ship has moved from one body of water into another. A strong 'fishy' smell has also been recorded associated with these displays that could be due to a large amount of dead plankton. Interestingly, with these displays it is impossible to get a sample, as any water that is taken by bucket cannot be induced to shine or flash light.

The causes of these ghostly displays are not really known. A possible cause could be waxes from the mass death of plankton, such as copepods, and the subsequent breaking up of their bodies. Bacteria, that can only be seen with a high-powered microscope, are the only organisms that can luminesce continuously and could be involved in the breaking up of dead organisms on a large scale. The Arabian Sea is often very rich in these bacteria in the summer months because of up-welling water caused by the monsoons and there is an increase in the amount of algae on the surface. Although the algae itself is not luminescent, it could be a base on which the bacteria can grow.

Luminescent Wheels

Luminescent wheels are waves of light travelling outwards very quickly in an expanding circle from a central hub, which may also be luminescent. The formation varies from 2m (6½ft) to 1.5km (1 mile) in diameter, and sometimes 'spokes' can be seen radiating from the hub to the rim. Some patterns revolve with either a constant direction, or they may change direction repeatedly. Wheels may start with an eruption of light from deeper water that explodes on the surface and spreads out in a large circle; at other times there may be many wheels, interlocking or separate. These wheels are mainly found in shallower water, and almost exclusively in the Indian Ocean and South China Sea.

Luminescent wheels are perhaps some of the most puzzling of all bioluminescent observations. Some have tried to explain wheels in terms of a ship's wake and waves, but this is not satisfactory. Records from hydrographic survey ships have reported bands of light resulting from using an air-

ABOVE When a sea pansy like this *Renilla* is handled, waves of light travel over and across the colony that is probably a defence against predators as the sudden 'fireworks' could either frighten a predator or temporarily blind one.

gun for taking seismic profiles of the sea bed, with light flashes coinciding with the firing of the gun. So perhaps the wheels are caused by seismic disturbances on the sea bed, which stimulate large numbers of plankton. But there have been no direct measurements of seismic activity or of the luminescent plankton in the relevant areas, nor has it been demonstrated that such seismic activity can stimulate organisms to luminesce.

Luminescent Bands

These displays of light have been reported in and around the Arabian Sea and Persian Gulf and the South China Sea, the Gulf of Thailand and Malacca Straits, with occasional reports from off the West African coast, South Africa and Ecuador. The display may be associated with a large luminescent wheel, as it is sometimes difficult to distinguish between the spokes of a large wheel and a system of bands. While sailing across this display, the vessel may appear to be sailing over a series of parallel lines that may be moving. Bands have been recorded passing at rates of between two and five per second. The lines are usually 100 – 400m (330 – 1,300ft) long, or may even stretch to the horizon; and they vary from 1.5 – 60m (5 – 200ft) wide and 0.5 – 300m (2 – 1,000ft) apart. The bands have distinct edges that distinguish them from streaks caused by winds or currents, or trails caused by flying fish or dolphins swimming. Such streaks or trails are shorter, less structured, and not as persistent. Again, a possible explanation may lie in seismic activity, although the evidence is not conclusive.

Erupting Luminescence

The phenomenon of erupting luminescence has been reported from the same locations as bands and wheels, with which they are often associated. Descriptions of them are often dramatic, with balls of light erupting from the depths to explode on the surface, before fading away if a wheel is not formed. The size of the ball varies between 30cm (12in) and 3m (10ft) diameter before spreading into a disc 30m (100ft) across. These are not the same as blobs of light seen in a ship's wake, which are the result of a collision with some unfortunate animal. Erupting luminescence is characteristic of deeper water and may again be associated with seismic disturbances.

Patches and Speckles

Small pinpricks of light in the water happen everywhere. Night divers get first hand experience with lights coming from their hands and fins as they swim though the water. These are caused by tiny life forms being disturbed and their colour, size and duration varies with species. Speckles can often be

seen among the more spectacular displays mentioned above. You can often find the animals, still glowing, sticking to your skin after a midnight dip and you can even write your name in light.

When a light beam is shone on the sea you can sometimes see tiny golden orange/yellow lights darting about. These are reflections from the eyes of fish and should not be confused with bioluminescence.

Bioluminescent Life Forms

Practically every animal group in the marine world has some species that can produce light.

Bacteria are well known on both land and sea to cause luminescence, but small planktonic animals, jellyfish, sea-gooseberries, some squid, many of the crustaceans such as the shrimps and krill, and even fish can produce different types of light displays. The colours and brightness of these lights vary slightly, but they are usually white, or sometimes a bright blue sapphire colour – very rarely red and yellow have been seen – and depend on the species, and indeed the brightness will depend on how much ambient light is present. Thus a dark, moonless night can produce some of the most spectacular displays.

RIGHT Many animals in the marine world can produce luminescence, though why the light is produced is often easier to answer than how it is stimulated, and it remains one of the great mysteries of the blue oceans. In the author's experience, while sailing in the Arabian Sea, we suddenly came across parallel bands of luminescence, passing the ship almost at right angles. A sample of water revealed a collection of bioluminescent siphonophore bells, which was not a surprise in itself; but why the luminescence was found in the band structures still evades explanation.

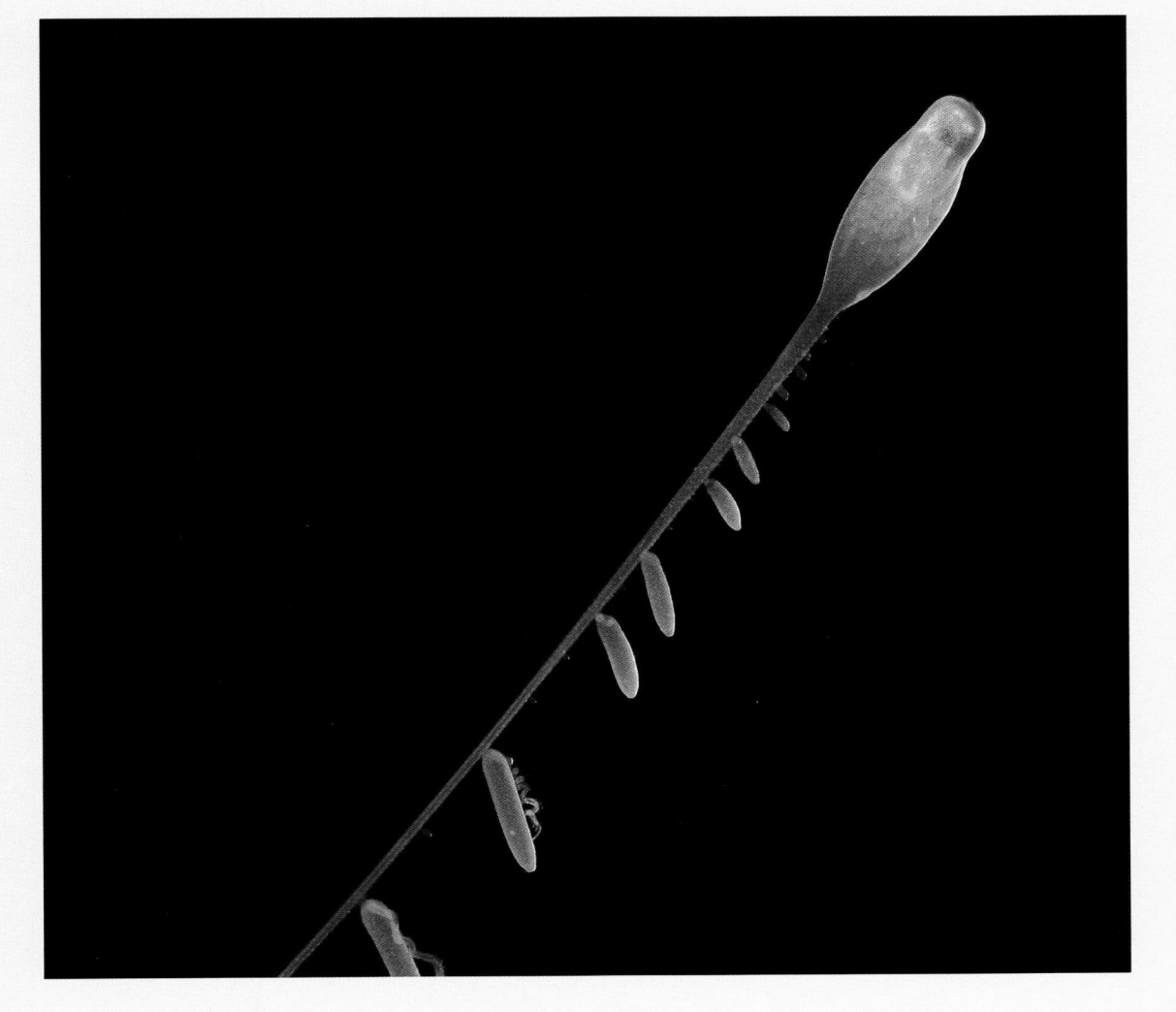

How the Light is Produced

Living organisms produce light in two ways. Most luminous fish have a substance called luciferin in special skin glands called photophores which have a clear window-like cover, a lens and a reflective layer. Some transparent animals have photophores inside their bodies.

When the luciferin is oxidized, the light released is reflected by the silvery reflective backing layer through the lens to give a fine beam. The second way that light is produced involves luminous bacteria that glow continually. To emit light, the bacteria need oxygen, and angler fish are thought to control the amount of light by altering the blood supply carrying oxygen to the tips of their lures. Some fish use black shutters that can flash the light on and off like a lighthouse, or they can send out a steady beam. By using different patterns of light flashes and beams, the luminous fish have evolved signals designed to alarm, attract, repel, guide or simply shed light on other creatures that dwell in the depths. Whether the luminescence is continuous, or in flashes or pulses, is a good clue to which animal is responsible. Although the stimulus that is needed varies, mechanical disturbance is the most common cause, and this may be caused by swimming, a

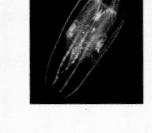

LEFT The arrangement of photophores on the underside of a fish, such as this midshipman, *Porichthys*, may act as camouflage. Predators looking up from below will then not be able to distinguish the fish from the surrounding light coming down from the surface, whereas a dark shadow would stand out clearly. Skin pigments, reflective surfaces, transparency and behaviour such as vertical migration in the water column add to the camouflage.

ABOVE Male and female lantern fish have different arrangements of luminescent organs or photophores along their lower sides which is clearly a way to identify members of the opposite sex in the deep dark world of the oceans.

OPPOSITE Many fish and squid have luminescent bacteria in hollows, but the bacteria's continuous light is undesirable so it is covered with a flap of skin, like an eyelid, when the light is not needed, such as in this flashlight fish.

passing ship, seismic activity, or just by shaking a jar of plankton; even organisms colliding with one another or with the sides of a container may cause luminescence. However, in all cases the light is caused by a chemical reaction, although the particular chemicals may differ in different species. In many small organisms the reaction takes place inside the body and the whole animal will light up; in others the chemicals are squeezed into the surrounding water to react, so producing a luminescent cloud. Many larger animals, such as the lantern fish or hatchet fish, that during the day are in deeper waters, have the luminescent photophores on their bodies where the chemical reaction takes place.

Although bioluminescence is a world-wide phenomenon, dramatic displays are mostly seen in productive tropical and sub-tropical waters. Bioluminescence can only be seen at night for several reasons: many bioluminescent animals are found in deeper waters during the day but migrate to the surface at night; the light during the day is not bright enough for bioluminescence to be seen; and some forms of bioluminescence may be inhibited by light.

Deep-sea fish themselves tend to be red coloured, which means they appear completely dark in the dim blue/black of deeper water. The velvety scales of these fish reflect no light, and so they are practically invisible in their natural habitat, except for the light from their photophores.

The Reasons Why

The ability to produce light is clearly beneficial, as so many animals have this capability. The blue-green light produced penetrates furthest in seawater, and most of the animals have eyes so this light can be detected.

There are a range of explanations for the production of light by animals and probably more to be discovered:

A Lure

Light can act as a lure to attract food. Many fishermen working at night hang lights over the sides of their boats to attract fish. In deep water, the angler fishes have a light on the end of an extension rather like a fishing rod, which dangles in front of their mouths. Some other fish have photophores on the inside of their mouths or cheeks which possibly attracts small inquisitive animals.

A Warning

A light may flash a warning to predators not to eat a particular animal because it is poisonous or nasty in some other way, such as having spines. The midshipman fish, *Porichthys*, is luminescent and has a poisonous spine, jellyfish are able to sting and the sea-gooseberries may just be unpleasant to eat. Some species may imitate types of luminescence even if they are not distasteful and so avoid being eaten as the predator associates a particular kind of light display with an unpleasant organism. A flashing light may also be a warning to others that a predator is nearby. Such a warning might not prevent the individual animal being eaten, but could benefit the species. Also a predator's enemies may be alerted by a flashing light. For instance, a large fish could be attracted to a flashing animal being eaten by a smaller fish, which then could become the prey of the larger animal. A predator may also use a flash of light to confuse any prey it is about to attack.

An Escape

A flash can startle a predator so that the prey can swim off in the dark. Some lantern fish have a light organ on their tails that flashes when they are being chased and copepods squirt out a cloud of luminescence before darting away. This may serve to temporarily 'blind' a predator. One species of deep sea squid has a luminescent 'ink' which it pumps out to confuse an attacker. In a contrary way, some fish switch off their photophores when they are attacked, which again leaves their predator 'blinded' and themselves virtually invisible.

Recognition

Animals that live in shoals can use lights to recognise each other. Some species can be distinguished by the arrangement of their photophores and perhaps the animals themselves also recognise each other in this way. It is also possible that in a world of darkness, light is the only way of telling other animals to keep out of a territory, so flashing a light may mark territorial boundaries. Each kind of lantern fish and hatchet fish, for instance, has its own particular pattern of lights along the underside of the body which are visible from a distance of about half a metre in dark water.

Sexual Display

Recognising your own species and opposite sex is vital for mating so some males and females have different arrangements of photophores and, in one fish species only males have photophores to attract females. Many animals increase their luminescent displays during the mating period, for instance, euphausiid shrimps normally respond to disturbance, but will respond to other light flashes during the breeding season; some ragworms luminesce during their breeding swarms, indeed some animals may carry out luminescent courtship displays.

Yet the reasons behind many types of bioluminescence remain a mystery. Why, for example, do deep water starfish have a variety of light-producing organs under their arms so the light is hidden? In others, a series of flashes passes down each arm, and in some, the light emanates from the organs in the central body of the animal. Mysterious it may be, but it is certainly impressive.

OPPOSITE TOP In the dark, a torch is clearly valuable to find your way around or, in the case of marine animals, to find food. Many *Euphausiid* shrimps can rotate their photophores so that they point forwards; the snout of the lantern fish has a large luminous disc that throws a beam of light on the krill on which it feeds.

OPPOSITE Squid and cuttlefish can produce some of the most sophisticated displays, with colours and light shimmering down the body that acts both as camouflage and defence. This is a Hawaiian bobtail squid, *Euprymna scolopes*.

ABOVE Some crabs live permanently among the weed while others, such as some of the swimming crabs, are just visitors. The species shown here, *Portunus sayi*, is a permanent resident within the Sargassum weed, but one that can make occasional forays into the surrounding water to hunt for other animals in the weed.

way through the tangled mat. Like most angler fish, it eats other fish, although it is not particular about its food, and shrimps are fair game. It will even consume its own kind – one fish that was caught was found to have sixteen smaller Sargassum fish in its stomach!

Like the frog fish, the Sargassum pipefish, *Syngnathus pelagicus*, which can easily be mistaken for a snake, is well camouflaged. The pipefish is greyish brown with speckled or indistinct white crossbands with black margins. This fish also has a dark longitudinal stripe in front of each eye, a cylindrical body up to 17cm (6¾in) long, with a tail fin that ends in a point. Like its cousin the seahorse, after the eggs are fertilized the male pipefish carries them in a brood pouch that runs along the belly; this pouch opens to the outside via a long slit to release the small fish when they hatch.

Visitors

The Sargasso Sea occurs in the central area of the rotating Atlantic Ocean currents. The east-bound north equatorial current marks the southern edge of the area, while the western and northern edge is formed by the north-east bound Gulf stream.

The waters in the Sargasso Sea are a calm deep blue, a part of the ocean where there is not much mixing, so the amount of nutrients is low. Consequently, the amount of animal life is low. But the Sargasso weed provides something of an oasis – a temporary home and food source for other animals in what would otherwise be something of a desert. There is a clear boundary between the weed community and the open sea.

A Temporary Home

Sailing or drifting around the Sargasso Sea on the ocean's surface are animals such as by-the-wind sailor, *Velella velella*, and the Portuguese Man-of-War, *Physalia physalis*, and their predator, the violet bubble-raft-snail, *Janthina*. *Porpita*, or sea button, is another drifting surface animal rather like the by-the-wind-sailor but much smaller, with small club shaped tentacles and no sail. As would be expected, these passive drifting ocean animals are often found in the weed. The oceanic sea slug, *Glaucus atlanticus*, may also be found hitching a ride.

Some other animals don't just drift into the Sargasso weed, but actively seek it out. Turtles, for example, spend some of their 'lost years' travelling with and feeding on floating Sargassum beds. Several fish such as the dolphin fish, *Coryphaena hippurus*, and members of the jackfish family such as the pilot fish, *Naucrates ductor*, use the Sargassum weed for shelter and hiding. Some flying fish lay their eggs in nests built from the weed.

LEFT This small floating sea fir or hydroid, *Porpita*, the sea button, is a circular raft about 8cm (3in) in diameter that can often get caught up among the Sargassum weed. The small translucent blue animal catches its prey on the club-shaped tentacles.

OPPOSITE The by-the-wind-sailor, *Velella*, lives on the ocean surface, blown along by the wind in its sail. It is rather like an upside down anemone with its tentacles beneath the raft. They can occasionally become tied up among the Sargassum weed.

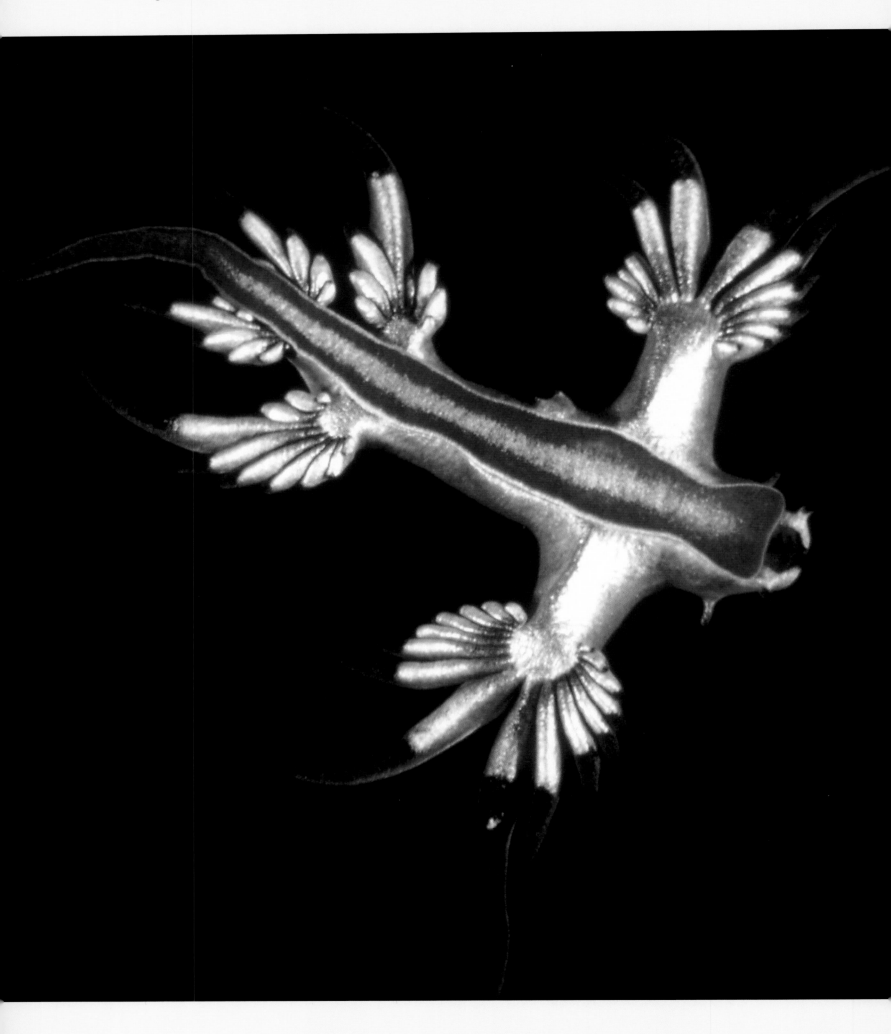

When looked at underwater, it appears that there are layers in the Sargassum community, perhaps rather like people in flats or apartments in cities. Those living in the penthouse are very closely associated with the weed and are mostly the permanent members of the community, including small fish such as filefish and triggerfish. Beneath the mat, perhaps a couple of floors down, are the larger, juvenile jacks while on the bottom floors, perhaps to the basement, are large predators, such as dolphin fish.

Common and Unusual Species

Some researchers call the Sargassum weed 'essential fish habitat', arguing that it provides a place for fish to spawn, breed, feed or grow to maturity. The weed is certainly an important nursery to several commercially important fish, and the young of bluefin tuna, billfish, as well as juvenile sailfish and amberjacks, are often found. Off the coast of North Carolina, the Gulf stream brings the Sargassum weed into the area, creating floating 'islands' that provide food and protection for huge numbers of fish – in fact, 81 fish species are known to use the weed.

One species of fish, which is extremely rare – so much so that there are only a couple of photographs available – is the oar fish, *Regalecus glesne*, so named because of its long oar-like pelvic fins.

The first account of the oar fish was in 1771 by a Danish naturalist, Morton Brunnich, who described a specimen that he found washed up on a beach in Norway – a long way from the Sargasso Sea. Since then, very few of these fish have appeared and it is probably not a permanent resident of the Sargassum weed community, but may occasionally be a visitor.

RIGHT Divers near the Bahamas recently saw this bright, elongated fish called an oar fish, *Regalecus glesne*. It has large eyes and two long antennae that appear to have diamond-shaped fishing lures along the lengths, and a large plume on its head. It propels itself through the water in an upright position by an undulating fin that runs the length of its back. Its body is thin and looks more like a long ribbon. The sight of this skinny 15m (45ft) long fish with its strange head covered in protrusions, among the weed, may go some way to explaining the old seafaring stories of serpents among the weed.

OPPOSITE The oceanic sea slug, *Glaucus atlanticus*, grows to 5cm (2in) long and normally glides along on the surface of the ocean. But it also is one of several of the oceanic surface drifters that can get caught up among the weed, though this does provide the potential for food, which is mainly other floating animals such as by-the-wind-sailor and the sea button.

CHAPTER NINE

INTO THE FUTURE...

While there is much to celebrate and wonder at in the oceans, there is also much to be concerned about as, unfortunately, the pace of discovering more about the abundance of life has often been outstripped by our technological capacity to take more, dump more and to essentially use the vast oceans and its wildlife simply as a resource to be exploited.

Recent decades have seen a welcome growth in awareness of what we have done and are doing to the planet. This has resulted in many international, regional and national laws that now ban some of the destructive practices in which we have thoughtlessly engaged in the past although worthy clauses on paper don't mean much without implementation, which remains a serious problem. But besides the legacy of past abuse, new threats and problems are being exposed which, arguably because they are less obvious and more insidious, pose a greater threat to the survival of the oceans, its wildlife and ultimately us.

The ocean world is a wonder, but it is not an infinite realm and there is much that we need to be concerned about.

A Limited Capacity

We have discovered, to our cost as well as a cost to ocean wildlife, that the ocean world is not infinite with a limitless capacity to absorb all the abuse that we give it. It is now clear that, when we throw things away there is, in fact, no 'away' – there is only here.

We are familiar with coastal waters because of their proximity and the varied use we make of them, but the deep oceans are relatively inaccessible and unexplored - we have better maps of the surface of the moon than of most of the seafloor. While coastal waters have national jurisdiction that has made some improvements, our impact on the oceans is not widely recognized. Perhaps it is too far away from the public eye and direct impact for the necessary attention. However, we are now beginning to realise that the high seas contain a rich variety of flora and fauna that is particularly vulnerable to human activities, because of the greater fragility of their ecosystems.

Today, the principle threats to the oceans come from fishing, the disposal of wastes (man-made structures, radioactive wastes, munitions and carbon dioxide), historical pollution, oil and gas extraction, marine mineral extraction and climate change. And while it is convenient to look at these individually, they interact in the fluid of the ocean ecosystem so their impacts need to be considered both directly and in relation to other influences.

A trawl through the history of our relationship to the oceans provides an important basis from which to build and provides an insight to how we have regarded the Earth. Today we question this insight – should we not view all the Earth and her inhabitants with respect and awe? Would such an insight not automatically lead to a greater degree of empathy and therefore concern?

Whaling

The history of industrial whaling, still serves as an object lesson in what happens when greed and laissez-faire industrial 'progress' is given free rein.

Native peoples have carried out whale hunting for at least 3500 years. For example, reports of Eskimo hunters date back to 1500 BC. These indigenous hunters worked, as they still do, from the shore and obtained food, clothing, weapons and lighting fuel from the whales.

Industrialisation

The start of the industrial revolution saw large sailing ships from England, Holland and America hunting whales mainly to get blubber for lighting. But with the development of steam powered bigger, faster ships and the invention of the explosive harpoon many more whales could be caught, including the largest and faster swimming rorquals, like the blue, fin and humpbacks. The industry grew rapidly in the late 19th and early 20th centuries as other commodities – fertilizers, medicines, tennis rackets, umbrellas, corsets, pet and human food – used whale products. Ambergris, a waxy aromatic substance produced by the sperm whale's digestion, was used in perfumes.

The advent of factory ships meant that catcher vessels need not tow their catch to shore, but could process it at sea. Thousands of whales were killed in the four month Antarctic season; in 1930, for example, 41 factory ships killed over 37,000 whales, nearly 28,000 of them blue whales; in 60 years an estimated 330,000 blue whales were killed.

Endangered Species

The blue whale was protected in 1966, though the industry had already turned to other species, as blues were getting too difficult to find. Repeating the pattern, in turn, the southern right, grey, fin, humpback and sperm whales all had to be protected.

Today the California grey whale is the only one thought to have recovered its numbers; by contrast the closely related West Pacific grey whale is hovering on the edge of extinction with just over 100 remaining. Antarctic blue whales are still less than 1 per cent of their original abundance and the total number of Antarctic whales is less than 10 percent of what it was before whaling began.

Exploitation v Subsistence

To the whaling industry, whales were a 'resource' to be sold – the more that were killed, the more money was made. Indigenous whalers, on the other hand, hunt whales (and seals and walrus) for their survival, only taking what they need. Over hundreds of years, the relationship between hunter and whale became cultural and based on respect. Indeed the respect for the environment often held by indigenous people could teach all of us much about our attitude to the Earth and its inhabitants. It was not native hunters that threatened the future of whales, but the greed fuelled by industrial societies.

Seals and Hunting

Seals and walrus have also suffered from heavy commercial exploitation ever since early traders realised that sealskins, blubber and meat could earn them money. Many species have been brought close to extinction, while earlier in the 20th century one species, the Caribbean monk seal, disappeared altogether. But once again it was the vast commercial exploitation that resulted in the need for protection, not indigenous hunting.

There is competition between seals and the fishing industry. On the one hand fishermen claim that culls are necessary, as the animals have reached such numbers that they are reducing fish stocks and damaging equipment. On the other hand there is insufficient information about the number of seals, their behaviour and effect on the industry to make such a judgement, although clearly increased fishing activity puts seals in direct competition. Further, although a fishing community may regard a particular species as too numerous in their locale, this could be one of the few remaining breeding sites in the world and a world view would show that numbers are actually low.

Today seals face threats of pollution, over-fishing, entanglement in debris and fishing gear and disturbance, so that the future of some seal populations remains precarious.

BELOW The development of the factory ship system so that whales could be processed at sea was devastatingly efficient, with thousands of whales being killed in each season. Today's equivalent is the fishing factory ship, unfortunately illustrating that lessons have not been learnt.

Fisheries

Unfortunately, the story of traditional harvesting of the seas turning to massive industrial expansion, followed by animals either being pushed into extinction or very close to the edge, is being repeated today.

According to the UN's Food and Agriculture Organisation (FAO), over three quarters of world fish stocks are either fully exploited or over exploited leaving only a quarter of fish populations that are currently being fished in a sustainable way. Excessive fishing leads to the collapse of fish stocks, which can alter nature's balance across vast areas of the world's oceans in ways that may be irreversible. This situation has remained unchanged over recent decades demonstrating the inadequacy of current fisheries management and proven by some spectacular fisheries collapses. For example, in 1992 the cod fishery collapsed off Newfoundland in Canada, leading to the loss of 40,000 jobs and today, the cod stocks in the North and Baltic Seas are close to complete collapse.

Unfortunately, fishing has turned into an unsustainable industry; as one stock is depleted, larger ships move further afield, leaving in their wake depleted fish populations and a ruined fishing community, as smaller vessels cannot travel too far from home. These practices endanger ocean ecosystems as well as the future of those dependent on the oceans for their livelihoods.

OPPOSITE Fishing is an ancient human tradition, one that satisfies the vital food needs of hundreds of millions of people and is economically, socially and culturally important in many poorer parts of the world. Today we have developed techniques that enable us to fish more intensively than ever before, with the result that tradition has been transformed into a resource extraction industry spanning the globe.

ABOVE The modern fishing industry is dominated by fishing vessels that far out-match nature's ability to replenish fish. Giant ships using state-of-the-art fish-finding sonar can pinpoint schools of fish quickly and accurately. The ships are fitted out like giant floating factories, containing fish processing and packing plants, huge freezing systems, fishmeal processing plants, and powerful engines.

Fishing for Whale Food

Krill, the major food for the great whales as well as penguins and seals, has also been fished, although recently the demand has dropped since its peak in the 1980s, when 480,000 tonnes (528,000 tons) were harvested. During the 2002/03 season, it is estimated that about 115,000 tonnes (126,000 tons) of krill were caught by fishing boats from Japan, Korea, Poland, Ukraine and the U.S. Today the krill fishery could grow again, as the world fish farming industry searches for sources of protein. Krill is also used in some pharmaceutical products and in 2003 there were 372 international patent applications for commercial uses of krill.

Deep-sea Fisheries

As coastal and surface waters become stripped of life, the industry looks ever deeper and farther afield. As seen in

Chapter 7, deep-water fish grow slowly and are long lived, which makes them more vulnerable to over fishing than those living on the continental shelf. If too many fish are caught before spawning age, the impact on future populations is catastrophic. The orange roughy, for example, which can live to well over 100 years and takes 20 – 25 years to mature, has been massively over-exploited in deep waters off New Zealand and Australia.

The Patagonian toothfish, which lives at depths of 3,500m (11,500ft) in the southern oceans, was only discovered commercially a decade ago. Like other deep-sea fish, it grows slowly, reaching spawning age in around 10 years, but with frozen toothfish selling at US$6 per kg (US$15 per lb) wholesale in New York, as compared with US$1 per kg (US$2.50 per lb) of fresh salmon, there is a flourishing illegal trade which threatens their survival: in 2003 toothfish sales in

LEFT Both the orange roughy and Patagonian toothfish are long-living deep-sea fish that are being destroyed by a massive and unsustainable fishing effort.

the US netted US$103 million. Currently over 100,000 tonnes (110,000 tons) are taken illegally and 10,500 tonnes (11,500 tons) legally. Intensive illegal fishing around the Prince Edward Islands south of South Africa has depleted the toothfish population to a few percent of its pre-exploitation level.

The recent development of fisheries around seamounts has been made possible by advances in the design of vessels, trawl gear and equipment that enables the sea floor to be accurately mapped and fish populations found. Deep-sea fishing is lucrative because the behaviour of congregating around seamounts provides large catches and over-exploitation of the populations happens within a very short time. For example, fishing of the pelagic armourhead over the Pacific seamounts northwest of Hawaii led to their commercial extinction in less than 20 years.

Destructive Fishing Techniques

Some fishing techniques, such as heavy bottom trawling destroy many fragile communities such as deep-sea corals. Other techniques like drift netting and long lining catch many non-target animals including marine mammals, turtles and seabirds. In the Southern ocean each year thousands of birds, such as petrels and wandering albatross, are killed as they get pulled under water after swallowing the bait on long-lines. Fishermen should use lines that sink before the birds can swallow the bait, but pirate fishermen ignore the regulations with the result that in 2003, 47,000 seabirds were killed in the

Southern Ocean. Drift netting is another technique that indiscriminately kills many species including dolphins, porpoises, turtles as well as sharks and non-target fish such as the sun fish.

Crews on illegal fishing boats are also endangered, as the vessels are often old and work outside safety and labour laws. At least three to four vessels are known to have disappeared in the last four years, taking about 100 people with them.

Farming fish has often been proposed as one answer to increasing the availability of fish. Unfortunately, fish farms produce a large amount of localised pollution from chemicals such as food additives and pesticides as well as the collection of huge amounts of uneaten food and fish excretions beneath the farms that uses up oxygen and kills seafloor communities. Further threats come from genetically modified fish and shellfish which could contaminate or modify wild populations.

Where fish stocks have collapsed, even complete closure of the fisheries has not resulted in regeneration and it is clear that other factors are operating. The destruction of the ozone layer, for example, could impact marine ecosystems, particularly in polar regions, by increasing the amount of UV-B radiation reaching the surface. Even the fundamental patterns of ocean circulation, which largely govern the earth's climate, could be changed due to global warming. Already there is evidence that plankton populations, which provide the basis for all life in the oceans, are changing in response to climatic changes.

The Oceans and Climate Change

Life on Earth is partly made possible by the greenhouse effect. If it weren't for the so-called greenhouse gases in the atmosphere, the temperature on Earth would be too cold for life to exist.

Greenhouse gases, mainly carbon dioxide, have built up in the atmosphere over millennia. These gases behave like the glass in a greenhouse in that they allow the sun's rays to pass through to the Earth, while simultaneously reflecting the heat from the ground back to the Earth, thus making the atmosphere warmer.

As with many things, too much of a good thing is bad. The fine balance of the Earth's atmosphere was fairly constant until the industrial revolution that was fired by the massive burning of coal and, subsequently, oil and gas, resulting in huge amounts of greenhouses gases being pumped into the atmosphere. At the same time we have destroyed huge tracts of forest that, like all plants, as part of Earth's balancing act, take in carbon dioxide as they grow. Today we continue to pump more greenhouse gases at the same time as removing the very things that take it out. This is warming the earth at a faster rate than at any time in human history.

The warming is melting glaciers and polar ice, warming the oceans and changing the climate. The resulting impacts are being felt world-wide with extreme floods and droughts as well as the spread of diseases now acknowledged by scientists as signals of a warming world.

In 1999 scientists expressed concern that global warming was impacting ocean ecosystems much earlier and more broadly than anticipated, and if warming continues, then

BELOW Global climate change is not just a warming world, but a disruption of entire weather systems leading to an increase in extreme events such as severe storms and flooding.

animals that depend on the ice-edge, such as many seals, Polar bears and walrus will be threatened by a reduction in habitat and food supply. Polar bears and walrus that rely on the ice edge for hunting have to wait longer for the ice to come at the onset of winter and search further for the ice edge in the summer. For walrus, which rely on shallow waters for food, this situation is serious.

The oceans drive our climate and weather, controlling the global deliveries of heat and fresh water. Climate change could cause major alterations in ocean currents. The nature of these changes, and their implications, are unpredictable, but some idea of the economic disruption that could be caused is shown by the El Niño phenomenon in the Pacific Ocean. This is a natural event where the cold current passing up the west coast of South America is suddenly switched off as a pulse of warm water from the central ocean penetrates further east than normal. In the 1997/98 El Niño, droughts, forest fires and air pollution were severe in some parts while floods and storms devastated other areas. Fisheries and agriculture were affected across the globe. If global climate change affects the movement of ocean currents, the changes would not only affect ocean productivity, but also could alter rainfall, temperature and weather patterns across the planet.

A discussion of climate change and oceans often focuses on rising sea levels caused by melting ice. However, the sea level is already rising globally at 1 – 2cm (¼ – ¾in) every ten years due simply to the fact that as the oceans warm they expand – warm water takes up more space than cold. This rate of sea level rise is predicted to double in the next century due to global warming. Rising sea levels have huge impacts especially for low-lying countries like many small island States in the Pacific and Indian oceans. Here whole nations and cultures are threatened with extinction as the encroaching sea contaminates fresh water and destroys homes.

Tropical and sub-tropical coral reefs are already victims of the warming oceans. They survive within a narrow temperature range; too cold and they won't grow, too warm and they die. Large areas of coral reef and atolls in the Indian and Pacific oceans have been bleached by increasingly warm water.

Pollution

Pollution takes many forms: agricultural run-off, nuclear and toxic industrial discharges and household waste. Ultimately all wastes we produce might end up in the oceans. Some waste dumping practices are now outlawed world-wide, but we have a legacy of years of abuse as some wastes end up back on the beach, while others remain a source of chronic pollution.

ABOVE Rubbish, particularly non-degradable materials such as plastics, take a significant annual toll on wildlife, from turtles to birds and mammals.

OPPOSITE The Arctic is warming faster than anywhere else on Earth. Walrus, one of many animals that rely on the ice edge, are threatened as the ice retreats further away over water too deep for them to dive for food.

While international regulations ban the dumping of radioactive and industrial waste in the sea (though some still challenge this), the pollution problems that are now coming to light are from more subtle and less obvious sources, such as the use of toxic antifouling paints on ships and oil and gas rigs that have impacted shallow water communities. Fortunately, these too are now the subject of international controls.

Marine pollution is a global problem affecting every ocean. Coastal seas near highly populated areas suffer discharges of fertilisers and chemicals from agriculture and industry that reach the sea via rivers, groundwater and the atmosphere. Pollution either kills living organisms directly or indirectly as predators eat contaminated life forms. But if not killed, then animals can become sicker and weaker making them more susceptible to natural diseases.

Some chemicals used in intensive agriculture and the food industries imitate hormones affecting the sexual organs and reproductive ability. Human sewage and nutrients from agriculture can stimulate blooms of marine algae, some of which produce toxins that kill shellfish, fish, sea birds and sea mammals. Litter from coasts and dumping rubbish at sea causes pollution, particularly by plastic materials. Turtles, which eat jellyfish, have been found with plastic bags in their bodies; a sperm whale found washed up dead in the Mediterranean had 50 plastic bags in its stomach.

There are about 63,000 different chemicals in use world-wide with many new synthetic chemicals brought onto the market each year, each with the potential to end up in the atmosphere and/or the oceans. Many are poisonous and remain in the environment for a long time. One group of the most serious pollutants are known as persistent organic pollutants or POPs which include pesticides such as DDT and Lindane, as well as highly toxic dioxins and PCBs (Polychlorinated Biphenyls). They do not degrade in the environment and they accumulate in the bodies of living organisms, including humans, particularly in fatty tissues,

disrupting hormones, resulting in reproductive problems, causing cancer, suppressing the immune system and interfering with normal cognitive development, particularly in the offspring.

POPs are also carried long distances in the atmosphere and deposited in cold regions. As a result, indigenous Arctic populations who live a long way from the sources of these pollutants, are among the most heavily contaminated people on the planet, since they rely on fat-rich marine food sources such as fish and seals. These chemicals are also thought to be responsible for reproductive failure in some polar bear populations.

Eating oily fish is one route where POPs are passed onto humans and other predators. But fish are also rendered down

ABOVE Because many chemicals stay and accumulate in the environment, they are often found a long way from where they were originally used. Persistent organic pollutants, or POPs, have been found in native people in the north, and are thought to be partly responsible for some polar bears failing to reproduce.

into fishmeal and fish oils and used to feed farmed fish, cattle, poultry and pigs, which is another route that these chemicals can reach humans.

Oil Pollution

Perhaps the most visible marine pollution is caused by tanker accidents and by tank washing at sea. Oil spills cause acute pollution to coastal communities and have long-term impacts.

For example, 15 years after the *Exxon Valdez* tanker ran aground in Prince William Sound, Alaska, biological impacts can still be identified. More recently *The Prestige* sank off the Spanish coast in 2002, resulting in huge economic losses as it polluted more than 100 beaches in France and Spain. Chronic pollution also results from oil and gas exploration and production where oil and toxic chemicals in wastewater and drillings smother the sea floor.

However, even today, some still look to the oceans to take our waste. One current threat is a proposal to use the sea as a dumping ground for greenhouse gases that could have profound and unpredictable impacts on ocean ecology. A far better and more reliable solution is to reduce greenhouse gas emissions in the first place by alternative energy and transport solutions as well as conserving and using energy more efficiently.

Deep-sea Mining

Much of the oil and gas from shallower parts of the oceans has been fully exploited so the oil industry is now expanding to deeper parts of the ocean and oil rigs now operate in water depths of 3km (1¾ miles). Such deep-sea operations threaten some of the most fragile communities in the oceans with habitat destruction and increased exposure to pollution either from accidents or the everyday operational discharges.

There are proposals to mine minerals such as metallic nodules from the deep sea and, while unlikely to be a commercial reality in the near future, it is an issue that needs to be watched closely. Our history of a less-than-benign attitude to the oceans shows that we need to remain vigilant.

ABOVE Oil spills cause huge amounts of local damage, and impacts can last a long time. Fifteen years after the *Exxon Valdez* ran aground in Prince William Sound, Alaska, there are still many impacts being felt on marine life. More recently, as shown here, the Spanish coast suffered a massive spill covering more than 100 beaches.

LEFT An oil rig is an enormous machine made from thousands of tons of steel welded together to form a platform on legs above the sea. Underneath, a gigantic drill plunges through the water, to penetrate the Earth's crust and extract crude oil. Chronic sources of pollution result from oil and gas exploration and production where oil and toxic chemicals in wastewater and drillings can disturb the sea floor, bottom-living communities and fisheries.

How can we Protect the Ocean World?

The oceans, like the atmosphere, are truly global. Currents flow around the world, irrespective of national boundaries and jurisdictions, so the consequences of activities in one area can really have global impacts. What can be done to ensure the ocean world is protected?

Much has been done, but there is more still to do; some things we can all do as individuals such as reducing the amount of waste we produce and reusing and recycling as much as possible. However, this responsibility must extend to corporate and industry level where, despite the acknowledgment of the problems caused by pollution, some continue to look to the oceans to take our waste, rather than trying to reduce its production in the first place.

As problems have come to the fore, despite resistance, national and international regulations have been agreed, but many of these need to be implemented. However, as industries such as fisheries and oil and gas exploration are greatly increasing their capacity to exploit areas and marine life that have hitherto been protected mainly through a lack of technical ability, more has to be done just to keep pace with the level of exploitation.

Marine Protected Areas

Establishing more marine reserves in key locations, such as in feeding and breeding grounds and on migration routes, is a vital step towards redressing the balance. Once set up, these would enable species to re-establish themselves in their natural environments, away from human interference. This would, in turn, allow sustainable fisheries to evolve. Of course, this wouldn't stop illegal activities, but it would make them more difficult to pursue. At the same time, it would allow for a more world-wide approach to the regulation of fish stocks.

This raises the problem of jurisdiction. Protected areas within a country's territorial waters are the responsibility of the national authority, but what of the open oceans outside of these waters? Who can police activities here? A further, deeper, question is how did we get to the point where ownership of areas appears to be the only way to protect them?

The Oceans: a Global Commons Approach?

The problems created by our abuse of the oceans have sometimes been called a 'tragedy of the commons'. In other words, while there is no regime to control activities, there is nothing to stop a whaler from going after the last whale; it does not pay for the fisherman not to go after the last fish. Neither does it pay for individual industries or governments not to take advantage of having coastlines to get rid of waste. The fisherman, whaler or industries get the benefit, but the cost is borne by all, including wildlife.

But to call this a tragedy of the commons would be wrong; it is a tragedy of a lack of common ownership and value. 'Commons' areas, as have been held by communities down through the ages – and still are today by some indigenous peoples – actually lead to greater protection because the commons benefits the whole community. Under commons regimes, no one individual is allowed to take more or do anything that would reduce the value or benefit of the commons to the community: witness commons grazing or use of forests by indigenous communities.

OPPOSITE AND RIGHT The oceans are a true global commons on which the natural world, including ourselves, relies. Being a commons, we all share responsibility for the protection and survival of all marine habitats and inhabitants, whether a green sea turtle on a stunning beach in Borneo or the people whose lives are still intimately connected with the sea.

Conclusion

So can we establish a global commons approach to the oceans? This would require a comprehensive and international approach to the protection of the oceans and deep-sea ecosystems from the full spectrum of human activities and impacts. We all need to take responsibility for protecting the global commons that is too valuable to be left to governments or industry.

Meanwhile, a moratorium is needed to stop some of the most damaging activities, such as destructive fishing practices. As such, a moratorium can be seen as a necessary but not sufficient management response to the totality of threats facing deep-sea biodiversity. It is vital that, alongside such immediate measures, much greater attention is given to the development of an effective and integrated system of marine protected areas.

While much has been discovered about the oceans and its wildlife, we are just getting a glimpse of the ocean realm. I hope this journey into the blue and back has provided a taste of the amazing world in the blue oceans. Once aware of these wonders, we cannot help but do all we can to protect this world which surrounds us and bathes the Earth and on which we all rely.

RIGHT Healthy seas, clean air and unpolluted land are vital for the survival of all the inhabitants of this wonderful blue planet.

The World's Oceans, Currents ar

ARCTIC OCEAN

GREENLAND

Norwegian

Hudson
Bay

Labrador
Sea

North Sea

EU

NORTH
AMERICA

North
American
Basin

Mid-Atlantic Ridge

Biscay
Plain

Med

Gulf of
Alaska

Aleutian Trench

Tufts Plain

Northeast
Pacific
Basin

Cape
Verde
Plain

Sargasso
Sea

Gulf of
Mexico

Middle American Trench

Puerto Rico Plain

Caribbean Sea

ATLANTIC
OCEAN

A F

Demeraro
Plain

PACIFIC OCEAN

Pacific Basin

SOUTH
AMERICA

Brazil
Basin

Angol
Plain

East Pacific Ridge

Peru-Chile Trench

Mid-Atlantic Ridge

Walvis Ridge

Southwest Pacific Basin

Southeast
Pacific Basin

Argentine
Plain

SOUTH
ATLANTIC
OCEAN

Atlantic-Ind

0

5000 Miles

0

5000 Km

ANTA

ajor Deep Sea Structures

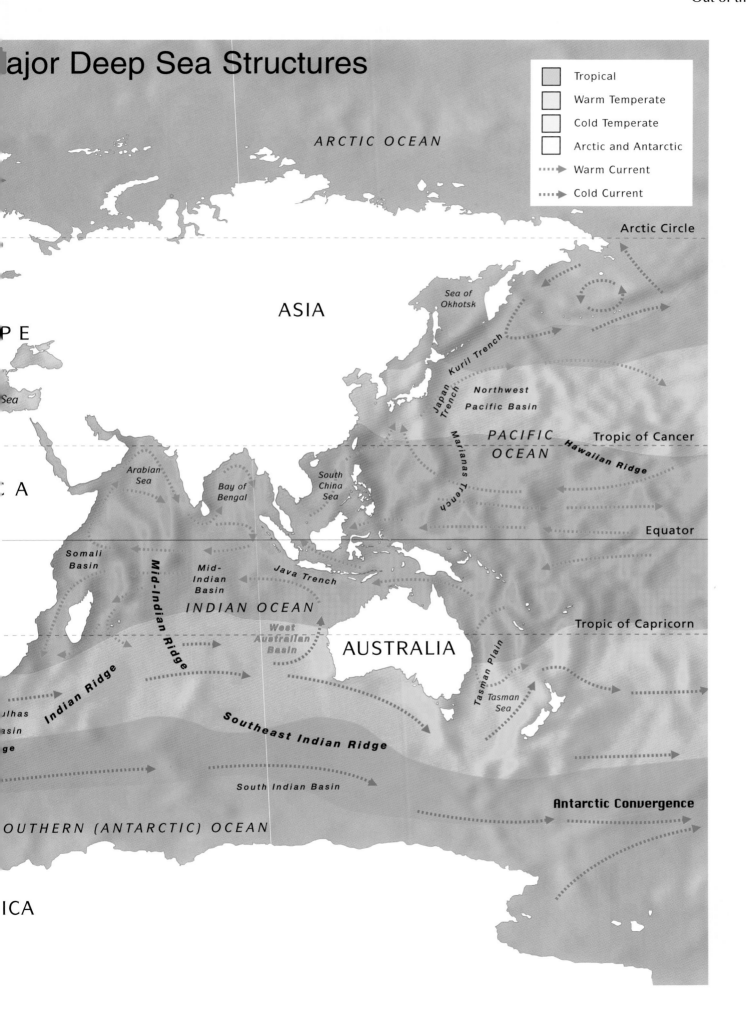

Tropical

Warm Temperate

Cold Temperate

Arctic and Antarctic

Warm Current

Cold Current

ARCTIC OCEAN

Arctic Circle

ASIA

Sea of Okhotsk

Kuril Trench

Japan Trench

Northwest Pacific Basin

PACIFIC OCEAN

Tropic of Cancer

Marianas Trench

Hawaiian Ridge

Sea

Arabian Sea

Bay of Bengal

South China Sea

Equator

Somali Basin

Mid-Indian Basin

Java Trench

INDIAN OCEAN

West Australian Basin

AUSTRALIA

Tropic of Capricorn

Mid-Indian Ridge

Tasman Plain

Tasman Sea

Indian Ridge

ulhas asin ge

Southeast Indian Ridge

South Indian Basin

Antarctic Convergence

OUTHERN (ANTARCTIC) OCEAN

ICA